THE TOP 100 FITNESS FOODS

THE TOP 100
FITNESS
FOODS

SARAH OWEN

DUNCAN BAIRD PUBLISHERS
LONDON

THE TOP 100 FITNESS FOODS
Sarah Owen

Distributed in the USA and Canada by
Sterling Publishing Co., Inc., 387 Park Avenue South, New York, NY 10016-8810

This edition first published in the UK and USA in 2009 by
Duncan Baird Publishers Ltd, Sixth Floor, Castle House, 75–76 Wells Street, London W1T 3QH

Managing Editors: Grace Cheetham and Deirdre Headon
Editor: Ingrid Court-Jones
Managing Designer: Suzanne Tuhrim
Designer: Jantje Doughty
Commissioned photography: Simon Smith and Toby Scott

Library of Congress Cataloging-in-Publication Data

Owen, Sarah.
 The top 100 fitness foods : 100 ways to supercharge your life / Sarah Owen.
    p. cm.
 Includes index.
 ISBN 978-1-84483-853-0
 1. Athletes--Nutrition. 2. Physical fitness--Nutritional aspects. I. Title. II. Title: Top one hundred fitness foods.
 TX361.A8O95 2009
 613.2'024796--dc22

                        2009018380

ISBN: 978-1-84483-853-0

10 9 8 7 6 5 4 3 2 1

Typeset in Helvetica Condensed
Color reproduction by Colourscan, Singapore
Printed in Malaysia by Imago

Notes on the recipes
Unless otherwise stated: • Use fresh herbs • 1 tsp. = 5ml, 1 tbsp. = 15ml, 1 cup = 240ml • Flours should be measured by
spooning, unsifted, into the cup and then leveled • All fruit and vegetables are medium-sized unless specified otherwise

For information about custom editions, special sales, premium and corporate purchases, please contact
Sterling Special Sales Department at 800-805-5489 or specialsales@sterlingpub.com.

CONTENTS

KEY TO SYMBOLS

 energy-boosting

 rehydrating

 joint-friendly

 bone-strengthening

 muscle-building

 stamina-improving

 blood sugar-balancing

 cramp-preventing

introduction

With soaring rates of obesity in the West, more people than ever before are taking responsibility for their own health and following a fitness routine or taking up a sport. Regardless of whether they're an absolute beginner or a world-class professional, all athletes have one thing in common—unique nutritional demands that require them to top up their energy tank with enough fuel to keep them going until the end of a game, a race, an aerobics class, or a gym session.

It's been proven time and time again that diet can have a significant impact on everything from speed and stamina to post-workout recovery rates. Here's what's needed to guarantee peak performance every time.

CARBOHYDRATE

Converted into glycogen, carbohydrates are the body's main source of energy and are stored in the muscles, where they're used as fuel during activity. Research shows regular exercisers need to consume approximately 50 to 60 percent of their total calorie intake in carbohydrates to maximize their performance.

One of the healthiest and most convenient sources of readily absorbed carbohydrates is fruit, which provides a quick energy boost, as well as helping to rehydrate the body. Unrefined grains, such as oats and brown rice, are rich in slow-releasing carbohydrates, which help feed the muscles steadily and sustain them for endurance events.

EAT TO STAY FIT

STAY HYDRATED

Of all the nutrients, water is the most important. It makes up more than 60 percent of body weight and is vital for the functioning of all cells. You need to top up your fluid levels regularly because water is lost through sweating, breathing, and urine, sapping endurance and strength. Even mild dehydration can result in fatigue, as the body is unable to cool itself efficiently, and losing the equivalent of 2 percent of body weight in sweat results in a 10 to 20 percent drop in aerobic capacity. Experts recommend drinking six to eight glasses of water a day, and possibly more in hot weather and during particularly intense bouts of exercise.

BEFORE EXERCISE

Research has found it's best to eat a light carbohydrate-based meal or snack two to four hours before exercise. This should leave enough time for the body to partially digest the food so you don't feel nauseous. The resulting rise in blood glucose levels allows the body to exercise harder and longer. Some studies also show that eating three hours before exercise helps the body to burn more fat. It's best not to eat a big meal just before working out, however, as that's likely to lead to performance-impairing sluggishness.

DURING EXERCISE

Anyone exercising for longer than 30 minutes benefits from sipping water periodically, while if a workout lasts longer than 60 minutes, studies have shown eating a high-carbohydrate snack can top up blood-sugar levels to help the body keep going for longer. Fast-burning carbohydrates, such as a banana or a granola bar, work particularly well. Isotonic drinks are also a good option—these carbohydrate-rich drinks provide fuel for the muscles and help to speed up the absorption of water into the bloodstream.

AFTER EXERCISE

Whether or not you feel hungry, the quicker you consume food or drink after a workout, the quicker your body will recover. The enzymes that make glycogen (muscle fuel) are most active between 30 minutes and two hours after exercise. Carbohydrate, in fact, is converted into glycogen one-and-a-half times faster than normal during this post-exercise window. If you wait more than two hours, the body's ability to reload muscle glycogen drops by 66 percent. Including a little protein in a snack speeds up glycogen recovery even more. Research shows the perfect post-exercise meal or snack is made up of three parts carbohydrate to one part protein —this ratio boosts glycogen storage by almost 40 percent.

USEFUL INFORMATION

• Each recipe serves four unless otherwise specified.

• Feel free to adjust the quantities and ingredients in the recipes to suit individual tastes.

• Wash all fruit and vegetables thoroughly unless they're organic, in which case a quick rinse under the faucet will do.

• Beans, especially kidney beans, can be poisonous if not cooked properly. Canned beans are a safe, nutritious alternative. If using dried beans, soak them for least five hours. Throw away the water and boil them in two to three times their volume of water 10 minutes. Drain, then cook them for at least one hour. Avoid slow cookers, which don't reach a high enough temperature to cook them thoroughly—undercooked beans are even more poisonous than raw ones.

• Green and brown lentils need to be soaked; red lentils don't.

• Always clean shellfish thoroughly, discarding any with shells that are broken or already open. Don't eat any that remain closed when cooked.

• Meat should be cooked through. Don't burn it, though, as this can create chemical reactions that have been linked with cancer.

PROTEIN

Protein is vital for the growth, formation, and repair of body cells and for making enzymes, hormones, and antibodies. It is also important for bone health.

Anyone who's physically active needs to eat more protein to make up for the increased muscle breakdown that occurs during and after exercise. The amount depends on the type of sport and intensity of the workout. Endurance athletes, such as long-distance runners, need 0.04 to 0.05 ounce of protein per 2lb. 4oz. of body weight; anyone who concentrates on strength activities, such as weight training, needs 0.05 to 0.06 ounce per 2lb. 4oz. of body weight a day. This is approximately 20 to 25 per cent of overall calorie intake for most adults. Excellent sources of protein include lean meat and poultry, fish, dairy products, legumes, soy, nuts, and seeds.

FAT

A concentrated source of energy, fat also provides the body with some important nutrients, such as vitamins A, D, and E. It's recommended most adults who work out or play a sport regularly should consume 20 to

25 percent of their total daily calorie intake in fat. It's worth remembering, however, that there are different types of fats, some of which are healthier for us than others. The so-called "bad" saturated fats (found in meat and dairy products) and hydrogenated fats (found in margarine, pastries, cookies, and fried food) have been linked to an increased risk of heart disease and stroke. Consequently, these should make up no more than 10 percent of the total calories most adults consume in a day. The remaining 10 to 15 per cent of our calorie intake from fats should be made up of "good" fats—the monosaturated fats (found in olives, avocados, and peanuts) and the omega-3, -6 and -9 essential fatty acids (found in fish, nuts, and seeds). These offer many benefits for athletes, including helping to reduce blood pressure and cholesterol levels, and working as an anti-inflammatory to protect joints.

VITAMINS AND MINERALS

Your body needs vitamins and minerals in minute amounts to help the body function at its best, and there's no doubt that getting the balance right boosts overall sports performance. Fresh fruit and vegetables are the richest sources of these important nutrients. Many vitamins, such as A, C, and E, are also antioxidants, which counterbalance the potentially damaging effects of free radicals produced naturally during exercise. It's recommended that anyone who works out or plays sports regularly consumes five to seven portions of fruit and vegetables a day.

pear

Bursting with natural sugar that converts easily into energy, a pear is an ideal pre-workout snack.

One pear contains approximately one-tenth of the recommended daily intake of potassium for most adults. This is important for anyone who exercises because a lack of potassium, which is a mineral easily lost through perspiration, can lead to fatigue and muscle cramps. Pears are also among the few fruits that contain lots of insoluble fiber, which works like tiny scrubbing brushes in the colon to promote good digestion.

NUTRIENTS
Vitamin C, beta-carotene, folate; calcium, iron, magnesium, phosphorus, potassium, zinc

POACHED PEARS

4 pears, peeled
scant ½ cup clear honey
½ cup apple juice
1 tsp. ground ginger
plain yogurt, to serve

Place the pears in a pan and pour the honey, juice, and 1 cup of water over. Sprinkle over the ginger and bring to a boil. Reduce heat, cover and simmer 20 minutes. Leave to cool in the syrup. Serve with plain yogurt.

Brown speckles on pears, known as russeting, indicate that they have a sweet flavor.

banana

The ultimate fast food, bananas provide a potent mix of vitamins, minerals, and carbohydrates.

Ripe bananas contain the ideal carbohydrate combination to replace muscle glycogen before or during exercise. Glucose, the most easily digested sugar, is immediately absorbed into the bloodstream for instant energy, while fructose is absorbed more slowly, providing a steady supply of fuel over a time. Bananas are also an excellent source of potassium and vitamin B6, which is involved in the manufacture of red blood cells as well as the breakdown of proteins, carbohydrates, and fats.

NUTRIENTS

Vitamins B3, B5, B6, C, K, beta-carotene, foliate; calcium, iron, magnesium, phosphorus, potassium, zinc

BREAKFAST SMOOTHIE *serves 2*

2 ripe bananas, peeled
20 raspberries
20 blueberries
2 cups plain yogurt
½ tsp. ground ginger

Whiz together the bananas, berries, and yogurt in a blender until smooth. Sprinkle over the ginger, and serve immediately.

plum

NUTRIENTS
Vitamins B2, C, beta-carotene;
copper, potassium

This versatile fruit can be eaten fresh or dried and is a useful source of immunity-boosting antioxidants.

Plums are rich in pectin, a type of soluble fiber that absorbs and neutralizes toxins in the large intestine, which means they have excellent detoxifying properties. They're great for helping to improve fitness in anemia-prone athletes because they're packed with iron, which is crucial in the formation of red blood cells. They also contain malic acid and the antioxidant vitamin C, both of which enhance the absorption of iron.

PLUM COMPOTE

16 ripe but firm plums
2 tsp. ground allspice
2 tbsp. dark brown sugar
1 cup plus 2 tbsp.
**   orange juice**
zest of ½ orange
plain yogurt, to serve

Place the plums in a large baking dish. Add the allspice, sugar, orange juice, and zest, and bake in a preheated oven at 350°F 30 minutes. Serve with plain yogurt.

peach

This deliciously sweet treat helps to prevent dehydration—a common cause of fatigue.

A 2-percent loss of fluid can cause a 20-percent drop in energy, which is why dehydration is one of the major causes of fatigue during prolonged exercise. As well as drinking plenty of water, eating foods with a high water content, such as a ripe, juicy peach, is a good way to top up fluids. Peaches also contain the trace mineral boron, which affects the way the body metabolizes calcium, making it important for healthy bones.

NUTRIENTS
Vitamins B3, C, beta-carotene, folate; calcium, iron, magnesium, phosphorus, potassium, zinc

PEACHY FROZEN YOGURT

**4 ripe peaches,
   peeled and stoned
10 raspberries
10 strawberries, hulled
1¼ cups plain yogurt
juice of ½ lemon**

Puree the fruit in a blender and place in a bowl in the freezer for 2 to 3 hours until semifrozen. Remove and whisk in the yogurt and lemon juice. Freeze again until firm. Remove from the freezer 30 minutes before serving.

Avoid buying peaches that have a green tinge, as they will never ripen properly.

lemon

NUTRIENTS
Vitamins B3, B5, B6, C, E,
beta-carotene, folate; calcium,
copper, iodine, iron, magnesium,
manganese, phosphorus,
potassium, selenium, zinc

Bursting with antioxidants, lemons make a great addition to any fitness diet, whether as a flavoring in cooked dishes, or simply squeezed over a salad.

Citric acid, which encourages healthy digestion, makes up 7 to 8 percent of a lemon—the highest concentration found in any fruit. Try diluting freshly squeezed lemon juice with warm water and drinking it on an empty stomach first thing in the morning. Lemon juice is also one of the most concentrated food sources of vitamin C, making it the ideal addition to a glass of water to help soothe a post-exercise dry throat.

LEMONY STUFFING BALLS   *makes 10*

1 small onion, quartered
1 egg, beaten
1 tbsp. rosemary
1¼ cups white breadcrumbs
juice and zest of ½ lemon

Whizz the onion, egg, and rosemary in a blender until smooth. In a bowl, mix the breadcrumbs with the lemon juice and zest, then add the onion mixture and mix well. Form into 10 small balls. Place on a baking tray and bake in a preheated oven at 350°F 25 minutes. Serve as an accompaniment to chicken or fish.

orange

The world's most popular citrus fruit is packed with infection-fighting and fat-burning nutrients.

Oranges contain natural sugars to help boost flagging energy levels and are full of vitamin C, a high intake of which can help to reduce post-exercise muscle soreness. They also provide citric acid, helping the body to absorb calcium, which is then stored in our fat cells. Oranges are a good source of the antioxidant hesperidin, thought to protect the heart by lowering cholesterol.

NUTRIENTS

Vitamins B3, B5, C, E, K, beta-carotene, folate; calcium, iodine, iron, magnesium, phosphorus, potassium, selenium, zinc

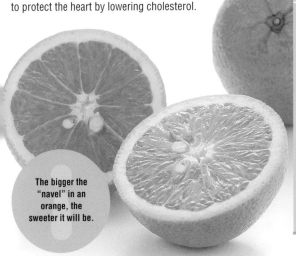

The bigger the "navel" in an orange, the sweeter it will be.

CHOCOLATE ORANGES

3½oz. dark chocolate, grated
1 tbsp. golden syrup or light
   corn syrup
zest of 1 orange
¼ cup light cream
4 oranges, peeled

Put the chocolate and syrup in a heatproof bowl and gently stir over a pan of simmering water. Once they are melted, turn off the heat and stir in the orange zest and cream. Divide the oranges into segments and arrange on plates. Drizzle the sauce over and serve.

star fruit

The exotic star fruit lives up to its name thanks to its powerful antioxidant properties.

Also known as the star apple or carambola, the star fruit is completely edible: as well as the small soft seeds found inside, the external skin can be washed and eaten, too.

NUTRIENTS
Vitamin C, beta-carotene, folate; potassium

STAR FRUIT FACTS
*The star fruit originates from Sri Lanka.

*Harvested when green, star fruit gradually turn a bright yellow, then a darker shade with brown tips when stored. This signals optimal ripeness, but doesn't impair texture or nutritional value.

*Anyone with kidney problems should avoid star fruit because of its oxalic acid content.

*In Chinese medicine, star fruit is known for its diuretic properties.

*In the Philippines, star fruit is eaten sprinkled with a little salt.

BOOSTS IMMUNITY
Nutritionally, the star fruit is a good source of disease-fighting beta-carotene. It is also packed with vitamin C, important for serious athletes because the body releases stress hormones into the bloodstream during heavy training, which can temporarily

SWEET-AND-SOUR NOODLES

10oz. egg noodles
2 tbsp. sesame oil
18 oz. cooked shrimp, shelled and deveined
4 small star fruit, sliced and tips removed
1 tbsp. soy sauce
juice and zest of 1 lime

Cook the noodles according to the packet instructions, then drain. Meanwhile, heat the oil in a pan until hot. Add the shrimp, star fruit, and soy sauce and stir-fry 3 minutes. Toss with the noodles and lime juice and zest, and serve.

suppress the immune system. Eating vitamin-C-rich foods counteracts this by significantly raising antioxidant levels.

CORRECTS FLUID RETENTION

Star fruit also contains potassium, which has a mild diuretic effect, promoting the elimination of excess water.

Star fruit bruises easily and needs very careful handling.

TROPICAL OAT COOKIES

¾ cup (1½ sticks) butter,
   plus extra for greasing
½ cup light brown sugar
scant ½ cup maple syrup
2 cups rolled oats
4oz sun-dried star fruit pieces

Melt the butter, sugar, and maple syrup in a pan, then mix in the oats and star fruit. Press the mixture into a greased 8-in. baking pan and bake in a preheated oven at 350°F 25 minutes. Leave to cool, then slice into squares.

fig

NUTRIENTS

Vitamins B3, B5, B6, C, beta-carotene, folate; calcium, copper, iodine, iron, magnesium, manganese, phosphorus, potassium, zinc

Among the best plant sources of calcium, figs are known as the bone-friendly fruit.

Figs are loaded with calcium, which is vital for strong bone density and particularly important for female athletes who train at high intensity. This is because they can experience low estrogen levels and amenorrhea, which increase bone loss and the need for calcium. Dried figs offer a concentrated burst of simple carbohydrate for instant energy, while fresh figs provide a unique, sweet taste and crunchy texture, and a higher dose of the vital antioxidant, vitamin C.

BAKED FIGS

12 figs, stems trimmed
1 cup walnut pieces
6 tbsp. maple syrup
1 tsp. cinnamon
plain yogurt, to serve

Cut a cross in the top of each fig and squeeze the fruit open. Place in a greased baking dish and sprinkle with the walnuts, maple syrup, and cinnamon. Bake in a preheated oven at 350°F 15 minutes until soft. Serve with plain yogurt.

date

Chewy, dried dates make excellent "survival food" on long bike rides or when hiking.

The ideal preparation for exercise is to eat a light meal three hours before you begin, and then to top up with a snack just half an hour before. Dates are the perfect snack option—they're high in carbohydrates for energy and an excellent source of potassium, which is important for maintaining the fluid and electrolyte balances in the body.

NUTRIENTS
Vitamins B3, B5, B6, C, K, beta-carotene, folate; calcium, copper, iodine, iron, magnesium, manganese, phosphorus, potassium, selenium, zinc

Dates can be frozen for up to a year in an airtight container.

FRUIT SQUARES

⅔ **cup dried dates**
⅔ **cup dried apricots**
½ **cup lime juice**
2 cups self-rising flour
½ **cup sugar**
3 eggs, beaten

Blend the dates, apricots, and lime juice in a food processor until smooth. Transfer to a large bowl and gradually mix in the flour, sugar, and eggs. Spoon the mixture into a greased 7-in. cake pan and bake in a preheated oven at 350°F 30 to 35 minutes. Leave to cool, then cut into squares.

mango

NUTRIENTS
Vitamins B3, C, E, beta-carotene; potassium

This sweet, juicy fruit provides an excellent vitamin boost and replaces essential minerals lost during a workout or match.

One 3½oz. serving of mango provides most adults with 60 percent of their daily vitamin-C needs, which helps the body heal faster from the aches, pains, bumps, and bruises that are often inevitable as a result of playing a sport. Mango is a good source of potassium, which is important for maintaining normal blood pressure. It is also one of the few fruit sources of vitamin E, shown to help speed up post-exercise recovery rates.

TROPICAL FRUIT SLUSH
serves 2

10 ice cubes
1 mango, peeled and roughly chopped
½ pineapple, peeled, cored and roughly chopped
10 strawberries, hulled
juice and zest of 1 lime

Whiz the ice cubes in a blender until slushy. Add the mango, pineapple, strawberries, and lime juice and zest, and blend until smooth. Serve and drink immediately.

In India, the mango tree is regarded as a symbol of love.

papaya

A daily portion of papaya can help prevent the "stitch", a sharp cramp in the side, which can occur during exercise.

Also known as pawpaws, papayas are packed with anti-inflammatory vitamin C, which helps to soothe overworked body tissues. They are rich in potassium, which is important for good fluid balance, and muscle and nerve function. Papaya also contain papain, a potent enzyme that encourages the elimination of waste products and reduces the risk of exercise-related stomach cramps.

NUTRIENTS
Vitamins B3, B5, C, beta-carotene, folate; calcium, iodine, iron, magnesium, manganese, phosphorus, potassium, selenium, zinc

THAI-INSPIRED SALAD

2 papaya, peeled and seeded
1 red bell pepper, seeded
10 scallions, chopped
1 cup bean sprouts
1 tbsp. sugar
1 tbsp. lime juice
1 tbsp. fish sauce
a handful mint, chopped

Dice the papaya and bell pepper into ½-in. cubes. Toss with the scallions, bean sprouts, sugar, lime juice, fish sauce, and mint in a large bowl, mixing well, and serve.

guava

NUTRIENTS
Vitamins B3, B5, B6, C, E,
beta-carotene, folate; calcium,
copper, iodine, iron, magnesium,
manganese, phosphorus,
potassium, selenium, zinc

The sweet-scented, creamy flesh of the exotic guava fruit makes it an ideal addition to a pre- or post-exercise smoothie.

With four times the vitamin C and 70 times the fiber content of an orange, the guava is a nutritional powerhouse that can help bolster the immune system. This is particularly important for regular exercisers, who use up their antioxidant reserves faster than non-exercisers. It is thought that the high fiber content of guavas lowers blood cholesterol by binding to it and eliminating it from the body.

GUAVA COULIS

12 ripe guavas, cut in half
1 cup powdered sugar
½ cup lime juice
½ tsp. vanilla extract
ice cream, to serve

Simmer the guavas in 1 cup water 8 minutes. Leave to cool and then push through a strainer into a pan using with the back of a spoon; discard the seeds. Add the sugar, lime juice, and vanilla extract to the pan and simmer 10 minutes, or until thickened. Cool and serve drizzled over ice cream.

lychee

Deliciously refreshing lychees are the perfect nutritious snack to have before exercise or between training sessions.

Light, rich in quick-energy carbohydrate, and easily digestible, lychees make an exotic change from other fruit bowl favorites. Available fresh, dried, or canned, nine lychees provide most adults' recommended daily intake of vitamin C and 15 percent more polyphenols (research shows these help keep the heart strong) than the equivalent number of grapes. To open a fresh lychee, score down one side with a sharp knife, peel off the crocodilelike skin and lift out the transparent, juicy flesh.

NUTRIENTS
Vitamins B1, B2, C; copper, potassium

Lychees are native to China, the Philippines, and India.

LYCHEE GEL

8 lychees, peeled, pitted
   and halved
½ mango, peeled and cubed
¼ cup sugar
¾oz. gelatin
2 cups apple juice

Place the lychees and mango in the bottom of four small serving bowls or molds. Heat the sugar in half the apple juice over a low heat until dissolved, then add the gelatin. Add the rest of the juice, pour over the fruit, and refrigerate overnight. Turn out onto plates to serve.

goji berry

Runners often nibble on dried goji berries to boost diminishing energy levels.

Research shows exercise increases the need for antioxidants, so goji berries are a great choice for athletes because they're rich in phytonutrients with significant antioxidant properties. Goji berries are also one of the few fruit sources of omega-3 essential fatty acids, good for keeping joints well-oiled. They are rich in amino acids to help improve stamina, and a complex phytonutrient called betaine, which is used by the liver to produce choline—a compound that promotes muscle growth.

NUTRIENTS
Vitamins B1, B2, B6, C, E, beta-carotene, folate; calcium, iron, phosphorus, potassium, selenium, zinc; omega-3 and omega-6 essential fatty acids

GOJI BERRY FRITTERS

1 cup dried goji berries
2 sweet potatoes, peeled
1 apple, peeled and grated
1 cup self-rising flour
2 eggs, separated
4 cups sunflower oil, for frying

Soak the goji berries in water 20 minutes, then drain. Chop the potatoes into 1-in. cubes, then boil 5 minutes, drain, and mash. Mix in the berries, apple, flour and egg yolks. Beat the egg whites until stiff and fold in. Deep fry dollops of the batter in hot oil for 8 to 10 minutes. Drain and serve.

Goji berries are also sometimes known as wolf berries.

avocado

Add this nutrient-packed fruit to salads or spread on bread to help boost strength and endurance.

A good source of healthy monounsaturated fat and loaded with 20 vitamins, minerals, and phytonutrients, avocados count among nature's true superfoods for anyone aiming to get fit. They contain more protein than any other fruit, making them great for strength and endurance. Just one avocado provides half most adults' recommended daily intake of vitamin B6—essential for helping the body release energy from food.

NUTRIENTS

Vitamins B1, B2, B5, B6, C, E, K, folate; copper, iron, phosphorus, potassium, zinc; carotenoids; monounsaturated fats

TANGY SUMMER SALAD

3 tbsp. olive oil
1 tsp. clear honey
1 red onion, grated
1 tsp. Dijon mustard
4 ripe avocados, peeled, pitted and sliced
1 pink grapefruit, peeled and segmented
large handful arugula leaves

Whisk the oil, honey, red onion, and mustard together in a large bowl. Add the avocados, grapefruit, and arugula leaves, toss well, and serve.

olive

NUTRIENTS

Vitamins E, K, beta-carotene; calcium, copper, iodine, iron, magnesium, manganese, phosphorus, potassium, selenium, zinc; omega-9 essential fatty acids

OLIVE FACTS

*The oil made from olives is one of the healthiest culinary oils, as it contains lots of monounsaturates, which are good for the heart.

*Olive oil is available in a variety of grades, which reflect the degree to which it has been processed. "Extra virgin" is the best choice, as it retains the most antioxidants.

*Store olives and olive oils in opaque tubs and dark, tinted bottles, as these help prevent the harmful oxidation caused by exposure to light.

Staples of Mediterranean cuisine, olives are bursting with health benefits for fitness fanatics.

There are hundreds of varieties of olive. Black olives tend to be moist and full-flavored, while green ones have a milder taste.

BEST FOR THE HEART

Olives are thought to keep the heart healthy because they're among the best sources of monounsaturated fats, which help lower harmfully high cholesterol levels.

PROTECTS JOINTS

Super-rich in vitamin E and omega-9 fatty acids, which have anti-inflammatory properties, olives also help to protect joints

---

OLIVE AND NUT DIP

1¾ cups pitted green olives
¾ cup walnuts, shelled
⅓ cup pine nuts
2 tbsp. grated Romano cheese
1 tbsp. olive oil
breadsticks, to serve

Whiz the olives, walnuts, and pine nuts in a blender until smooth. Mix in the cheese and olive oil. Serve with breadsticks.

from workout wear and tear. In addition, the essential fatty acids in olives have been shown to boost the body's ability to remove unwanted stored fat in the cells.

STRENGTHENS BONES
One recent scientific study suggests eating olives on a regular basis also plays an important role in protecting bones against osteoporosis.

MINI KEBABS
Makes 24

24 black olives,
  pitted and halved
24 cherry tomatoes, halved
48 basil leaves
7oz. feta, cut into 24 cubes
black pepper

Spear 2 olive halves, 2 tomato halves, 2 basil leaves and 1 cube of feta onto each of 24 cocktail sticks, alternating ingredients. Season with pepper and serve.

In the wild, olive trees bear fruit only every other year.

lettuce

NUTRIENTS
Vitamins B1, B3, B5, C, E, K, beta-carotene, folate; calcium, iodine, iron, magnesium, manganese, phosphorus, potassium, selenium, silica, zinc

A salad and sandwich staple, lettuce provides vital nutrients for helping the body make energy.

Lettuce contains many minerals, including iron, calcium, zinc, and magnesium, which play a role in the generation of energy. Equally important for an athlete's health is the folate content – this B-vitamin protects the heart by converting a damaging chemical called homocysteine into benign substances. If not converted, homocysteine can directly damage blood vessels, greatly increasing the risk of heart attack and stroke.

CHEESY BROILED LETTUCE

1 romaine lettuce
1 tbsp. olive oil
7oz. camembert cheese
2 tsp. balsamic vinegar

Cut the lettuce in quarters lengthwise, brush with the oil and broil 2 minutes on each side. Arrange in a shallow baking dish and top with thin slices of camembert. Drizzle the vinegar over and bake in a preheated oven at 425°F 5 minutes, or until the cheese is bubbling. Serve immediately.

The darker the color of the lettuce leaf, the higher its nutritional content.

bell pepper

Whether eaten raw as a crunchy crudité or softened in a stir-fry or roasted dish, sweet bell peppers pack a powerful nutritional punch.

After exercise, the body continues to burn fat. Bell peppers mirror this process because they contain substances that significantly increase heat production in the body for more than 20 minutes after they are eaten, helping burn calories quicker. One 5½-oz serving of bell pepper provides most adults' daily recommended intake of vitamin C and beta-carotene, which both have potent immunity-boosting antioxidant properties.

NUTRIENTS
Vitamins B3, B6, C, E, K, beta-carotene, biotin, folate; calcium, iodine, iron, magnesium, manganese, phosphorus, potassium, zinc

RED PEPPER SALSA

1 red bell pepper, seeded
  and finely diced
2 beef tomatoes, finely diced
½ small red chili pepper,
  seeded and finely chopped
1 small cucumber, finely diced
4 tbsp. chopped cilantro
juice and zest of ½ lime

Mix all the ingredients together in a bowl. Serve as a dip or a sauce.

beet

NUTRIENTS
Vitamins B3, B5, C, folate, beta-carotene; calcium, iodine, iron, magnesium, manganese, phosphorus, potassium, zinc

A high natural sugar content helps beet revive flagging energy levels on the playing field.

Not only do beets provide easily digestible sugars, but their dietary fiber also slows down the absorption of these carbohydrates into the blood, which means the body is supplied with a steady stream of energy. Beet juice is a concentrated source of the antioxidant betacyanin and, if drunk on an empty stomach, is an effective internal cleanser. Other great ways to introduce this vegetable into the diet include grating it raw into salads or slow-cooking it in soups and stews.

RAINBOW ROOT SALAD

2 large beets,
  peeled and grated
3 carrots, peeled and grated
1 parsnip, peeled and grated
1 red onion, grated
juice of 1 lemon
1 tbsp. olive oil

In a large bowl, mix all the grated vegetables well. Drizzle over the lemon juice and oil, and serve.

onion

Famed for adding flavor to savory recipes, onions boast incredible fitness benefits, too.

For anyone aiming to reach peak physical fitness, onions can offer several minerals, including chromium, manganese, and potassium, which help break down fat deposits and speed up metabolism. They are also full of quercetin (a flavonoid that is not destroyed during the cooking process), which has been shown to help reduce fatigue. Studies suggest that onions can help maintain healthy bones by inhibiting the activity of osteoclasts—the cells that break down bone.

NUTRIENTS
Vitamins B6, C, folate; chromium, copper, manganese, phosphorus, potassium

Onions contain sulfurous amino acids that boost the body's ability to detoxify.

CARAMELIZED ONION SAUCE

4 large onions, chopped
1 garlic clove, crushed
2 tbsp. olive oil
1 tsp. Dijon mustard
1 cup light cream
pasta, cooked, to serve

Cook the onions and garlic in the oil in a pan 45 minutes over a very low heat, stirring occasionally. Stir in the mustard, and cook 10 minutes longer. Stir in the cream. Serve with pasta.

pea

NUTRIENTS

Vitamins B-complex, C, K, beta-carotene, folate; copper, iron, magnesium, manganese, phosphorus, potassium, zinc

For weight-conscious sports players, peas are an excellent, quick-to-cook side dish.

Exceptionally rich in both soluble and insoluble fiber, peas are one of nature's best aids to weight control. Studies demonstrate that the more fiber we consume, the less likely we are to gain weight and the more readily we shed excess fat. Fiber has also been shown to have a positive effect on the hormones in the intestines that control appetite. In addition, the vitamin C and iron in peas help keep energy levels topped up.

PEA RISOTTO

1 onion, finely chopped
1 tbsp. olive oil
2 cups peas
¾ cup arborio rice
1 cup milk
3 cups hot vegetable stock
a handful mint, chopped
½ cup Parmesan cheese, grated

In a heavy-bottomed pan, fry the onion in the oil until golden. Add the peas and cook 2 minutes. Stir in the rice and milk. Gradually add the stock ½ cup at a time, stirring until absorbed before adding more. Cook for 20 minutes. Then, gently stir in the mint, sprinkle over the cheese, and serve.

An average portion of frozen peas contains the same amount of vitamin C as two large apples.

carrot

This versatile vegetable provides instant energy, fiber and a long list of health-boosting nutrients.

The highly concentrated sugars in carrots are easily absorbed for on-the-spot energy. Carrots are among the richest sources of beta-carotene, which is converted by the body into the antioxidant vitamin A, shown to help prevent heart disease and speed up post-exercise recovery time. Eating two carrots a day can help to reduce high cholesterol levels: nibble on raw sticks, drink the juice, chop into stews and soups, or grate into cakes.

NUTRIENTS

Vitamin C, beta-carotene, biotin, folate; calcium, iron, magnesium, manganese, phosphorus, potassium; bioflavonoids; limonin; lycopene; pectin

CARROT CAKE

½ cup (1 stick) butter
⅓ cup clear honey
1 cup brown sugar
1¾ cups plus 2 tbsp.
   wholewheat flour
1 tsp. baking powder
1½ cups peeled and
   grated carrots
1 tsp. ground cinnamon

Grease an 8-in. round cake pan. In a bowl, beat the butter, honey, and sugar together. Fold in the remaining ingredients, mix well, and spoon into the cake pan. Bake in a preheated oven at 350°F for 1 hour.

butternut squash

NUTRIENTS

Vitamins B1, B3, B5, B6, C, E, K, beta-carotene, folate; calcium, copper, iron, magnesium, phosphorus, potassium, selenium, zinc

Squash is a nutritional winner and is delicious in soups and stews, and with other roasted vegetables.

BOOSTS IMMUNITY

Like all orange fruit and vegetables, the butternut squash is a great source of beta-carotene, which the body converts to vitamin A, needed for a healthy immune system and good digestive and respiratory-tract function.

> You can tell if a squash is ripe by tapping it— if ripe, it will sound hollow.

SPICY ROASTED VEGETABLES

3 tbsp. sunflower seeds
1 tsp. ground chilli
1 tsp. cumin seeds
1 tsp. ground coriander
1 tsp. ground ginger
1 butternut squash,
  peeled and seeded
2 zucchini, chopped
1 red pepper, seeded
  and sliced
7oz. mushrooms, halved
3 tbsp. olive oil
1 tbsp. balsamic vinegar

Toast the sunflower seeds and spices in a skillet until golden. Chop the squash into 2-in. chunks and place with the other vegetables in a roasting pan. Add the oil and vinegar, and mix well. Bake in a preheated oven at 375°F 1 hour, stirring occasionally.

SUSTAINS ENERGY

A great provider of energy-sustaining carbohydrates, squash contains high levels of the minerals potassium and magnesium, which help maintain efficient energy production. A lack of these minerals can lead to fatigue, muscle cramps, and an increased risk of high cholesterol, high blood pressure, and heart problems. Squashes are also thought to reduce the symptoms of prostatic hyperplasia, a benign prostate condition.

BUTTERNUT SQUASH FACTS

*Archeologists have found evidence in Mexican caves to suggest humankind has been eating squash for at least 7,000 years.

*Butternut squash is a variety of winter squash. Other varieties of winter squash include acorn, spaghetti, and sweet squash.

*Winter squash develops more beta-carotene after being stored than it contains immediately after picking.

*The smallest butternut squashes are usually the tastiest.

cauliflower

Prevent a sluggish system slowing you down with this excellent internal cleanser.

A member of the nutritionally powerful cruciferous family of vegetables, cauliflower contains a compound called glucosinolate, which fuels and strengthens the liver in its job as detoxifier, cleansing the body for peak performance. Cauliflower is also a good source of the B-vitamins, the most important nutrients needed for energy production and to support the adrenal glands.

NUTRIENTS
Vitamins B3, B5, B6, C, folate; calcium, manganese, potassium, zinc

CURRIED CAULIFLOWER AND LENTILS

1 tbsp. olive oil
1 garlic clove, crushed
1 onion, finely chopped
1 tbsp. curry powder
1 cup hot vegetable stock
1 cauliflower, broken into florets
heaped ½ cup red lentils
brown rice, to serve

Gently heat the oil in a large pan. Add the garlic, onion, and curry powder and fry until soft. Stir in the stock, cauliflower, and lentils, then cover and simmer about 20 minutes. Serve with brown rice.

Anyone with gout should avoid cauliflower, as it contains purines, which help to form uric acid.

025

broccoli

Celebrated as a superfood, broccoli contains compounds that can boost motivation, helping to lift a fatigue-related mood dip.

The long list of nutrients in broccoli means it is a brilliant energy-reviver. The zinc enhances mental alertness, vitamin B5 helps the body metabolize fats into energy, and the folate encourages the production of serotonin, a mood-lifting chemical in the brain. A good plant source of calcium, broccoli also promotes post-workout muscle relaxation and has bone-building properties.

NUTRIENTS
Vitamins B1, B3, B5, B6, C, E, K, beta-carotene, folate; calcium, iodine, iron, magnesium, manganese, phosphorus, potassium, zinc

SPICY BROCCOLI

2 heads of broccoli, broken into florets
1 onion, finely chopped
2 tbsp. sunflower oil
1 tbsp. curry powder
½ tsp. ground chili
1 cup heavy cream
½ cup flaked almonds

Steam the broccoli until tender. In another pan, fry the onion in the oil until soft. Add the broccoli, spices, and cream. Simmer 5 minutes, then sprinkle the almonds over. Serve as a side dish.

corn

NUTRIENTS
Vitamins B3, B5, C, beta-carotene, folate; magnesium, phosphorus, potassium, zinc

Barbecued or boiled, corn is a crunchy and deliciously sweet accompaniment to meat.

Fresh corn, made up of the yellow or white kernels that grow on the cob, is the most nutritious way to eat corn, as it provides starchy carbohydrates and a vegetable source of protein for a steady stream of energy during exercise. Yellow corn is a good source of the potent antioxidant lutein, which promotes healthy vision and a strong cardiovascular system. When canned or frozen, corn retains most of its goodness.

CORN RELISH

2 ears of corn
¼ cup (½ stick) butter
1 red bell pepper, seeded and finely diced
1 red onion, finely diced
2 celery ribs, finely diced
½ cucumber, finely diced

Boil the corn in salted water 8 minutes until tender. Drain, slice off the kernels, and mix with the butter. Stir in the remaining ingredients. Serve as a condiment.

> To stop corn from burning on a barbecue, soak it in water for 10 minutes and wrap in foil before cooking.

chard

Eaten raw or cooked like spinach, chard is a valuable source of iron for non-meat-eating athletes.

A member of the beet family, chard has crunchy stalks and spinachlike leaves with a slightly bitter, earthy flavor. Chard is an excellent bone-builder thanks to its calcium, magnesium, and vitamin K content, which are all thought to aid bone mineralization. Many of the nutrients in chard keep blood vessels strong, allowing blood to move oxygen around the body easily to boost strength and energy levels.

NUTRIENTS

Vitamins C, K, beta-carotene, folate; calcium, iron, magnesium, zinc

CHARD WITH SESAME SEEDS

1 onion, chopped
1 tbsp. olive oil
1 tbsp. tamari sauce
¾ cup sesame seeds
10oz. chard leaves, sliced

In a pan, fry the onion in the oil until soft. Stir in the tamari sauce and sesame seeds. Add the chard and stir until wilted. Serve immediately.

bok choy

NUTRIENTS
Vitamins B2, B6, C, beta-carotene, folate; calcium, iron, magnesium, manganese, phosphorus, potassium, selenium, zinc

Crank up the nutritional content of stir-fries and spring rolls with this potent Chinese vegetable.

Bok choy belongs to the cabbage family and has a mild, mustardy taste. Both the leaves and stalks are edible and packed with nutrients. Baby leaves with very fine stalks work brilliantly in salads. One average portion of cooked bok choy contains the same amount of calcium as ½ cup of whole milk. Bok choy also has an abundance of vitamin C, which aids recovery from sports injuries by strengthening cell walls.

CRUNCHY VEGETABLE STIR-FRY

1 tbsp. sesame oil
1 onion, finely chopped
1 garlic clove, crushed
½ cabbage, shredded
2 cups sliced mushrooms
4 bok choy, shredded

Heat the oil in a wok over high heat. Add the onion and garlic and stir-fry 2 minutes. Add the cabbage, mushrooms and bok choy and stir-fry 4 minutes longer, or until tender. Serve immediately.

Bok choy is also known as pak choi and Peking cabbage.

mushroom

Sugar cravings, whether they occur before, during or after exercise, can be tamed by including mushrooms regularly on the menu.

Mushrooms are a slow-release energy food thanks to their high content of vegetable protein. They're also especially rich in chromium, which helps stabilize blood-sugar levels and, in turn, helps control sugar cravings. The older you are, the less likely you are to be taking in enough chromium. Mushrooms are also an important source of vitamin B12 for vegetarians, which is vital for maintaining healthy energy levels.

NUTRIENTS

Vitamins B1, B2, B3, B5, B6, B12, E, folate; calcium, chromium, copper, iron, manganese, phosphorus, potassium, selenium, zinc

MUSHROOM PÂTÉ

13oz. chestnut mushrooms, chopped
2 tbsp. olive oil
1 tbsp. soy sauce
7oz. mascarpone cheese
2 tbsp. chopped tarragon

In a pan, fry the mushrooms in the oil 2 minutes. Add 4 tablespoons water and simmer 10 minutes. Leave to cool, then drain and puree the mushrooms. Add the remaining ingredients. Refrigerate 1 hour, then serve with toast.

okra

NUTRIENTS
Vitamins B1, B3, B5, B6, C, K,
beta-carotene, folate; calcium,
iodine, iron, magnesium,
manganese, phosphorus,
potassium, selenium, zinc

If training is disrupted due to an upset stomach, okra can help your digestive system recover.

This vegetable, which looks like a mini green banana, is a staple in Middle Eastern cooking and regularly features in Indian, North African and Caribbean cuisines. Okra is a good source of soluble fiber, which helps reduce cholesterol and stabilize blood sugar levels. It also contains psyllium, which acts as a probiotic in the gut, encouraging the growth of friendly bacteria and helping soothe stomach upsets.

VEGETABLE GUMBO

14oz. okra, stems removed
2 zucchini, trimmed
2 yellow bell peppers, seeded
3 beef tomatoes
1 onion, finely chopped
1 tbsp. sunflower oil
1 tbsp. tomato paste
brown rice, to serve

Chop the vegetables into 1-in. cubes. In an ovenproof dish, fry the onion in the oil, then add the vegetables and cook until soft. Mix in the tomato paste, cover, and bake in a preheated oven at 375°F 1 hour. Serve with brown rice.

Because of their shape, okra are commonly known as ladies' fingers.

sweet potato

An oven-baked sweet potato is the perfect light meal for anyone who prefers the gym to the kitchen.

Despite its sweet taste, this root vegetable provides healthy complex carbohydrate, releasing a steady stream of energy into the bloodstream and helping regulate blood-sugar levels. An antioxidant powerhouse, sweet potato is an excellent source of vitamins C, E, and beta-carotene, which work synergistically with one another to ward off post-workout fatigue. It also contains vitamin B6 to help protect the heart.

NUTRIENTS
Vitamins B1, B3, B5, B6, C, E, beta-carotene, folate; calcium, iodine, iron, magnesium, manganese, phosphorus, potassium, selenium, zinc

STEAMED SWEET POTATOES AND SNOW PEAS

**3 sweet potatoes,
    peeled and diced**
3oz. snow peas
3 tbsp. soy sauce
1 tbsp. sunflower seeds

Place the potatoes in a Dutch oven. Add 2 tablespoons water, cover, and steam 8 minutes until tender. Stir in the snow peas and cook 2 minutes longer. Transfer the vegetables to a bowl, and sprinkle with the soy sauce and sunflower seeds. Serve as a side dish.

yam

A fabulous form of slow-releasing energy, this starchy root vegetable is a more fitness-friendly alternative to the potato.

Thanks to their rich fiber content, yams rank lower on the glycemic index and provide a more sustained form of carbohydrate energy than the more popular potatoes.

BOOSTS ENERGY

High in potassium and low in sodium, yams help regulate the fluid balance that exercise can so easily deplete through perspiration. Yam contains several of the B-vitamins and is

NUTRIENTS
Vitamins B1, B3, B5, B6, C, E, folate; calcium, iodine, iron, magnesium, manganese, phosphorus, potassium, selenium, zinc

YAM FACTS
*One of the most widely consumed foods in the world, yams have been cultivated since 8,000BCE in Africa and Asia.

*Yams come in yellow, white, ivory, and purple varieties.

*There are more than 200 species of yam.

*Yams sometimes have offshoots, known as "toes."

*Unlike sweet potatoes, yams are toxic if eaten raw although both are perfectly safe to eat when cooked.

CITRUS YAMS

2 yams, peeled and chopped
   into 1-in. chunks
4 tbsp. olive oil
1 tbsp. chopped parsley
1 tbsp. chopped cilantro
juice and grated zest of
   1 orange
juice and grated zest of 1 lime

Steam the yam for 20 minutes until tender. In a bowl, whisk together the oil, parsley, cilantro, and orange and lime juices and zest. Fold the cooked yam into the dressing and mix well. Serve as an appetizer, a side dish, or a snack.

particularly rich in vitamin B1, useful for boosting energy levels, and manganese, a trace mineral that helps with the metabolism of carbohydrates and aids the formation of connective tissue.

BALANCES BLOOD SUGAR AND SALT

Discoretine, another chemical found in yam, is particularly useful for athletes, as it reduces blood sugar and increases blood flow through the kidneys. This promotes the excretion of excess salt, which, in turn, helps reduce high blood pressure.

Never try to eat the skin of a yam, as it is woody and inedible.

YAM DUMPLINGS ROLLED IN POPPY SEEDS

2 yams, peeled and chopped
3 egg yolks
½ tsp. ground chili
2 tsp. cornstarch
3 tbsp. self-rising flour
4 tbsp. poppy seeds

Boil the yam 20 minutes until tender. Drain and leave to cool, then puree in a food processor. Transfer to a bowl and mix in the egg yolks, chili, cornstarch and flour. Form into balls and roll in the poppy seeds. Line a steamer with foil and place over a pan of simmering water. Steam 10 minutes, then serve.

eggplant

NUTRIENTS

Vitamins B1, B3, B6, C, K, beta-carotene, folate; calcium, copper, iodine, iron, magnesium, manganese, phosphorus, potassium, selenium, zinc

Thanks to its high number of healing compounds, eggplant helps to ward off many performance-impairing illnesses.

Eggplants are loaded with antioxidants, including chlorogenic acid, which is antiviral, antibacterial, and antifungal, and nasunin, a flavonoid found to mop up free radicals, protecting the body against diseases. A member of the nightshade family, eggplants should be avoided by sufferers of osteoarthritis as they can increase inflammation in the joints.

EGGPLANT AND RICOTTA CHEESE ROLLS

1 large eggplant, trimmed
3 tbsp. olive oil
juice and zest of 1 lemon
7oz. ricotta cheese
4 sun-dried tomatoes, chopped
black pepper

Cut the eggplants lengthwise into ¼-in. thick slices. Coat in the oil, lemon juice and zest. Then, spread out on a baking tray and griddle 3 minutes each side. Put some of the cheese, tomato, and black pepper on each slice. Fold up and spear with a toothpick. Griddle 2 minutes, then serve.

grape leaves

Commonly used in Greek cuisine, grape leaves contain flavonoid antioxidants to help prevent post-exercise muscle soreness.

Tender, dark green grape leaves, with a subtle flavor and texture similar to spinach, are available both fresh and ready-to-use in brine. Like all leafy green vegetables, they contain flavonoids and vitamin C, useful for anyone working out regularly because a diet rich in antioxidants has been shown to promote faster recovery after exercise and to help the body stay in peak condition.

NUTRIENTS
Vitamin C, E, K; calcium, iron, magnesium, manganese, phosphorus, potassium, selenium, sodium, zinc

STUFFED GRAPE LEAVES

14oz. ground lamb
1 cup long-grain rice
a handful mint, chopped
1 tbsp. olive oil
1 tbsp. finely chopped
   scallions
salt and black pepper
16 grape leaves

Mix the lamb, rice, mint, oil, and scallions in a bowl and season with salt and pepper. Place 2 grape leaves on top of each other, add a dollop of the rice mixture, and roll to form a parcel. Repeat to make 8 parcels. Place in a steamer over a pan of simmering water. Steam the parcels 1 hour, or until tender, and the meat and rice are cooked.

Boil fresh grape leaves in salted water 4 minutes before using them.

crayfish

NUTRIENTS

Vitamins B3, B12; calcium, copper, magnesium, potassium, selenium, sulfur, zinc

Freshwater crustaceans, crayfish are loaded with immunity-boosting minerals.

Crayfish look like miniature versions of lobsters, to which they are closely related. They are an excellent source of selenium, an antioxidant mineral that research shows is one of the best natural cell-protectors around, as it mops up the free radicals produced by the body during exercise. A selenium deficiency is associated with anxiety, depression, and fatigue. Crayfish is also a valuable source of zinc, which helps ward off disease.

CRAYFISH TAGLIATELLE

10oz. fresh tagliatelle
18oz. cherry tomatoes, halved
1 tbsp. olive oil
juice and zest of 1 lemon
a handful basil leaves
14oz. cooked crayfish tails

Cook the tagliatelle in a large pan of salted boiling water 6 to 8 minutes, or as instructed on the package, then drain. In another pan, cook the tomatoes in the oil 5 minutes. Add the lemon juice and zest, basil, crayfish, and tagliatelle. Serve immediately.

trout

With a third of the fat of salmon, trout is an excellent alternative for the calorie-conscious.

Trout is a good source of essential fatty acids, which have been found to help increase an athlete's speed, because they improve the delivery of oxygen to the body's cells, boosting energy levels and building stamina. Omega-3 fats have also been found to stimulate production of a hormone called leptin, which helps control appetite. In addition, trout is packed with protein to encourage muscle growth and repair.

One 3½-oz. portion of trout contains just 135 calories.

NUTRIENTS
Vitamins A, B1, B2, B6, B12; calcium, iron, selenium; omega-3 essential fatty acids

TROUT STUFFED WITH HERBS

4 fresh whole trout, gutted and cleaned
a handful sage
a handful rosemary
juice of 2 lemons
¼ cup (½ stick) butter
steamed greens, to serve

Line a baking tray with foil and place the trout on it. Stuff some herbs into each fish and drizzle each with the lemon juice. Melt the butter and pour it over the fish. Bake in a preheated oven at 350°F 35 minutes. Serve with greens.

salmon

NUTRIENTS

Vitamins A, B3, B6, B12, D, E, folate; calcium, magnesium, phosphorus, selenium; omega-3 essential fatty acids

SALMON PATTIES

½ cup long-grain rice
18oz. salmon fillets, boned skinned and chopped
1 onion
1 egg
1 garlic clove, crushed
2 tsp. sunflower oil, plus extra for frying
1 tbsp. roughly chopped cilantro
1 tsp. salt

In a pan, bring the rice and ½ cup water to a boil, then simmer for 10 minutes and leave to cool. In a blender, puree the onion, egg, garlic, and oil. Mix well with the salmon, rice, and cilantro and form into 8 patties. Fry in oil 4 to 5 minutes each side and serve.

One of the healthiest forms of protein, bone-friendly salmon is a superb choice for athletes.

If regular exercisers are not getting enough protein in their diet, they take longer both to recover after training and to build up their muscles and stamina. Salmon provides plenty of protein, as well as one of the highest levels among all foods of omega-3 essential fatty acids and DHA (docosahexaenoic acid), both of which are renowned for helping to reduce post-exercise joint stiffness. DHA is especially important for helping blood flow smoothly through the arteries.

tuna

Tuna provides a low-fat, protein-packed nutritional hit that's quick to prepare.

Lean sources of protein are key for anyone who's physically active, as they prevent slumps in energy without sending calorie intake soaring. Like other oily fish, fresh tuna is exceptionally rich in omega-3 fatty acids, which play an important role in energy production and helping to burn excess fat. Flash-cook thin slices of tuna on a preheated ridged skillet or, for an even speedier option, use canned varieties.

NUTRIENTS

Vitamins B1, B3, B6, B12, D, E; iodine, magnesium, phosphorus, potassium, selenium, sodium; omega-3 essential fatty acids

Look out for albacore, skipjack, and yellowfin tuna, which are the most nutritious kinds.

TUNA AND GREEN BEAN SALAD

4oz. green beans, steamed and chopped
4oz. cherry tomatoes
2 tbsp. olive oil
14oz. tuna steaks

In a bowl, toss the beans with the tomatoes and oil. Broil the tuna 3 minutes each side. Slice, arrange over the salad, and serve.

sardine

NUTRIENTS
Vitamins B3, B6, D, E; calcium,
iodine, iron, potassium, selenium;
omega-3 essential fatty acids

Being one of the few nondairy sources of easily absorbable calcium makes sardines a first-rate food for athletes.

Including plenty of calcium in the diet is essential for strong bones and, according to the latest research, can also help the body burn body fat. Sardines are packed with protein, iron, zinc, essential fatty acids, and vitamin D, and are exceptionally rich in calcium. Ask the fish merchant to remove the heads and backbones, but leave the other bones—once cooked they're very soft and you can just mash them with a fork.

JAPANESE SARDINES

1lb. sardines, gutted,
    cleaned, and dried
½ cup soy sauce
¼ cup white wine vinegar
juice and zest of 1 lime
1-in. piece ginger root,
    peeled and chopped
2 garlic cloves, crushed
1 lemon grass stalk, chopped
1 tsp ground chilli
green salad, to serve

Arrange the sardines in a shallow dish. Mix together the remaining ingredients and pour over the sardines. Cover and refrigerate 3 hours. Discard the marinade and broil the sardines 3 to 5 minutes, turning once, until the flesh flakes. Serve with a green salad.

Canned sardines
are an inexpensive,
highly nutritious
"instant" food.

mackerel

Put fresh, smoked, or tinned mackerel on the menu to guarantee a host of health and fitness benefits.

Mackerel fillets are simple to cook and easy to digest. They're loaded with omega-3 essential fatty acids, which help prevent heart disease and keep joints healthy, while their vitamin E content helps protect the nerves and heart from the wear and tear of sport. Mackerel is also one of the few food sources of vitamin D (usually manufactured in the body from sunlight), which, along with the calcium, is crucial for good bone health.

NUTRIENTS

Vitamins B3, B6, B12, D, E; calcium, iodine, potassium, selenium; omega-3 essential fatty acids

MACKEREL MASH

4 potatoes, peeled and diced
2 tbsp. butter
1 tbsp. milk
1 tbsp. chopped parsley
2 shallots, finely chopped
14oz. cooked mackerel fillets, skinned and flaked
black pepper
green salad, to serve

Cook the potatoes in a large pan of salted, boiling water until soft. Mash with the butter and milk. Stir in the parsley, shallots, mackerel, and pepper. Serve with a green salad.

pollack

NUTRIENTS

Vitamins B3, B12; calcium, iodine, magnesium, potassium, selenium; omega-3 essential fatty acids

It's firm, white, flaky flesh makes pollack a delicious, nutrient-packed substitute for cod.

As global stocks of cod become seriously depleted, pollack is rapidly becoming an increasingly popular alternative.

INCREASES ENERGY

One 3-oz. portion of pollack provides more than 20 percent of the recommended daily intake of energy-boosting selenium and

> Pollack is a prime low-fat source of protein, containing less than 5 percent of fat in its flesh.

POLLACK CHOWDER

1 tbsp. olive oil
1 onion, chopped
3 carrots, peeled and diced
2 large potatoes, peeled and diced
heaped ½ cup brown rice
2 cups vegetable stock
18oz. pollack, boned, skinned and cut into 1-in. chunks
¼ cup milk
wholewheat rolls, to serve

Heat the oil in a pan. Add the onion and fry lightly. Add the carrots, potatoes, rice, and stock, and bring to a boil. Reduce the heat and simmer 15 minutes. Add the fish chunks and milk and simmer 8 minutes longer. Serve immediately with wholewheat rolls.

vitamins B3 and B12 for most adults, as well as more than 10 per cent of their recommended daily intake of magnesium and potassium, which balance the level of fluid in the body. Pollack is also rich in iodine, a mineral needed to regulate the metabolism and the activity of the thyroid gland.

REBUILDS MUSCLE

A fantastic source of lean protein, pollack helps the body feel full for longer, especially when eaten with carbohydrate, such as brown rice. This combination also aids the repair of muscle because the carbohydrate triggers the release of the hormone insulin, which acts like a key, opening the cells to allow them to absorb the amino acids contained in the protein.

POLLACK FACTS

*When fresh, pollack never smells fishy, the eyes appear bright and clear, and the flesh "gives" slightly when pressed and then springs back into shape.

*To store pollack, remove the packaging, rinse under cold water, and pat dry with paper towels. Place on a cake rack in a shallow pan filled with crushed ice. Cover with plastic wrap and set in the coldest part of the refrigerator.

*If it's well-wrapped, pollack can be frozen for 3 to 4 months.

shrimp

The world's most popular and versatile crustacean, shrimp work well in sandwiches, salads, stir-fries, and seafood stews.

NUTRIENTS
Vitamins B3, B12; calcium, iodine, magnesium, phosphorus, potassium, selenium, sodium, zinc

Shrimp are packed full of vital minerals, including potassium, magnesium, and sodium, which all help restore an athlete's electrolyte balance after a heavy training session. As shrimp are higher in sodium than most foods (although not in harmful levels), they can also help prevent the mineral imbalance that can result from drinking too much water during an energetic workout.

> Shrimp bought with their shells on have a better flavor than those already shelled.

SHRIMP AND BULGUR WHEAT

1 cup bulgur wheat
2 cups hot vegetable stock
1 red onion, finely diced
14oz. cooked shrimp, shelled
2 large handfuls of basil
  leaves, chopped

Place the bulgur wheat in a pan, pour the vegetable stock over and leave to stand 30 minutes. Stir in the onion, shrimp, and basil, and serve immediately.

oyster

This delicious shellfish delicacy provides protein, B-vitamins, and a massive dose of minerals.

The highest natural source of the mineral zinc, oysters are great for boosting immunity and improving the quality of sperm. A great source of energy for athletes, oysters are an excellent form of low-fat protein. They also contain vitamin B12, which helps to prevent pernicious anemia, and iodine, vital for the proper functioning of the thyroid gland, which, if underactive, can lead to seriously debilitating bouts of exhaustion.

NUTRIENTS
Vitamins A, B3, B12, C, D, E; calcium, iodine, iron, magnesium, selenium, zinc; omega-3 essential fatty acids

ROASTED OYSTERS

16 fresh oysters
1 tbsp. sesame oil
1 tbsp. white wine vinegar
1 tbsp. lemon juice
2-in. piece ginger root, grated
1 tsp. salt
wholewheat bread, to serve
butter, to serve

Place the oysters deep-shell down on a baking tray and bake in a preheated oven at 400°F 5 minutes, or until they open. Whisk the oil, vinegar, lemon juice, ginger, and salt in a bowl. Flip off the top shells and drizzle the dressing over. Serve in their shells with wholewheat bread and butter.

044

mussel

Crammed with joint-protecting essential fatty acids, muscles are a great food for anyone who regularly pounds the pavement.

An average portion of mussels provides most adults with half their daily recommended intake of omega-3 fatty acids, which are known for their anti-inflammatory properties, helping keep joints well oiled, and preventing common sports injuries. Mussels are also very rich in zinc, a mineral essential for the breakdown of carbohydrates, fats, and proteins into energy.

NUTRIENTS
Vitamins B2, B6, B12, E, folate; calcium, iron, magnesium, potassium, selenium, zinc; omega-3 essential fatty acids

SEAFOOD SALAD

10oz. cooked and
  shelled mussels
4oz. cooked and
  shelled shrimp
1 onion, grated
½ white cabbage, shredded
2 carrots, peeled and grated
1 medium beet, peeled
  and grated
2 tbsp. mayonnaise

Mix the mussels, shrimp, onion, cabbage, carrots, and beet in a large bowl. Mix in the mayonnaise and serve.

scallop

A type of mollusc with a soft, fleshy texture and a delicate, mild flavor, scallops are loaded with heart-friendly nutrients.

Scallops provide four nutrients that have significant cardiovascular benefits for sportsmen and -women—vitamin B12, omega-3 essential fatty acids, magnesium, and potassium. Vitamin B12 is needed by the body to counteract homocysteine, a chemical that can directly damage blood vessel walls; omega-3 fats help the blood flow smoothly; magnesium encourages blood vessels to relax, lowering blood pressure; and potassium aids in the maintenance of normal blood-pressure levels.

NUTRIENTS

Vitamin B12; calcium, magnesium, phosphorus, potassium, selenium; omega-3 essential fatty acids

BROILED CILANTRO SCALLOPS

24 scallops, shelled and shells reserved
½ cup (1 stick) butter
juice of ½ lime
small a handful cilantro, finely chopped

Place the scallops flesh-side up on a baking tray. Broil 2 minutes. Divide the butter, lime juice, and cilantro into the shells. Broil 2 to 3 minutes longer until the scallops are cooked through, then serve.

The edible part of the scallop is known as the "nut."

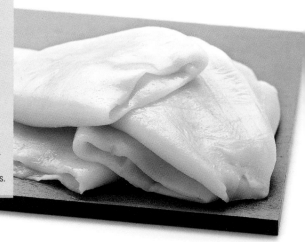

squid

NUTRIENTS
Vitamins B2, B3, B6, B12; calcium,
iodine, magnesium, manganese,
phosphorus, potassium, selenium,
zinc; omega-3 essential fatty acids

With its distinctive, sweet taste, squid meat contains higher levels of immunity-boosting zinc, manganese, and copper than many other seafood.

Scientists have found that the proteins contained in squid meat are the same kinds of proteins found in fish meat, and are equal in nutritional value. With virtually no saturated fat, eight essential amino acids, and a high level of easily digestible protein, squid is a good way for exercisers to get the increased protein they need to compensate for the increased muscle breakdown that occurs during and after intense exercise.

SALT AND PEPPER SQUID

1 tbsp. salt
1 tbsp. peppercorns
4 tbsp. cornstarch
4 tbsp. semolina
18oz. squid, tubes and
   tentacles, cut into
   bite-size pieces
4 cups vegetable oil,
   for deep-frying
mayonnaise, to serve
lemon wedges, to serve

Crush the salt and pepper
with a mortar and pestle and
mix with the cornstarch
and semolina. Toss the squid
in the mixture to coat. Fry in
hot oil until golden, then drain.
Serve immediately with
mayonnaise and lemon wedges.

cod roe

Loaded with nutrients as well as tasting delicious, cod roe makes a fitness-friendly topping for toast.

Made up of the eggs of the female fish, cod roe is a wonderful source of vitamins D and E, containing almost as much vitamin E as an equivalent portion of wheat germ (the highest plant source of vitamin E). The omega-3 fatty acids provide all the raw materials the body needs to produce anti-inflammatory compounds that soothe post-workout aches and pains, and the protein slowly releases energy to drip-feed the muscles after an exercise session or sports match.

NUTRIENTS
Vitamins A, B1, B2, B3, C, E; calcium, iron, magnesium; omega-3 essential fatty acids

COD ROE ON TOAST

14oz. cod roe
3 tbsp. all-purpose flour
2 tbsp. olive oil
a large handful arugula leaves
4 slices of wholegrain bread, toasted and buttered
juice of ½ lemon

Cut the cod roe into ½-in. slices. Lightly coat in the flour and gently fry in the oil 3 minutes on each side. Arrange the arugula leaves on the wholegrain toast. Add the cod roe, drizzle over the lemon juice, and serve.

A 6-oz. portion of cod roe provides more than double the daily requirement of vitamin D for most adults.

beef

NUTRIENTS
Vitamins B1, B2, B3, B6, B12; iron, phosphorus, selenium, sulphur, zinc; omega-3 essential fatty acids

HOMEMADE HAMBURGERS

scant ½ cup long-grain rice
1 small onion
1 egg
a pinch salt
12oz. lean ground beef
1 tbsp. olive oil
wholewheat buns, to serve

In a pan, cook the rice in ½ cup water. Puree the onion, egg, and salt together in a food processor. In a bowl, mix the beef and cooled rice thoroughly with the egg mixture. Mold into burgers. Fry in the olive oil 7 minutes on each side, or until cooked as desired. Serve in wholewheat buns.

An excellent source of protein and iron, beef helps anyone who's physically active stay fighting fit.

The body's iron stores are depleted through perspiration, plus the impact of the feet hitting the ground when running destroys red blood cells, which means it's common for athletes to be deficient in this important mineral. Beef is a rich animal source of iron, which is easier to absorb than plant sources. It also contains conjugated linoleic acid, which stimulates the conversion of stored fat into energy.

The healthiest, leanest cuts of beef are topside, sirloin, and filet steak.

lamb

Protein-rich lamb helps prevent hunger pangs on the pitch or track, or in the studio or gym.

A lamb shank or loin is a lean cut of meat loaded with protein, which helps suppress the appetite longer and prolongs satiety more than foods high in carbohydrate or fat. Lamb is also rich in the mineral sulfur, a key component of chondroitin sulfate, a complex molecule that gives cartilage the elastic, spongelike quality joints need to act as shock absorbers between the bones.

NUTRIENTS

Vitamins B1, B2, B3, B6, B12; iron, phosphorus, selenium, sulfur, zinc

BAKED LAMB AND POTATOES

1lb. 2oz. new potatoes
8 bay leaves
2 red onions, sliced
2 tbsp. olive oil
juice of 1 lemon
a handful mint, chopped
8 lamb loin chops

Put the potatoes, bay leaves, and onions on a baking tray. Sprinkle with a little of the oil and the lemon juice. Cover with foil and roast in a preheated oven at 425°F 40 minutes. In a pan, brown the chops on both sides in the remaining oil. Remove the foil from the potatoes, add the chops and mint, and roast 15 minutes longer, then serve.

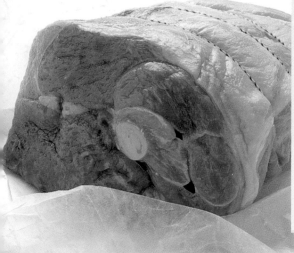

pork

NUTRIENTS
Vitamins B1, B2, B3, B6, B12; potassium, selenium, zinc

Pork is a valuable source of two trusty energy providers—protein and the B-vitamin complex.

While eating in general raises the metabolic rate, protein boosts it the most: up to 20 percent of a protein meal's calories can be burned off. An average portion of pork (3 to 4 ounces) contains 1 ounce of pure protein. It also has a full house of B-vitamins, which are essential for converting carbohydrates into energy and preventing fatigue.

ROAST GAMMON WITH PLUM GLAZE
serves 8

½ cup plum jam
juice and zest of 1 orange
1 tsp. ground nutmeg
1 tsp. cinnamon
1 tsp. ground ginger
5lb. gammon roast

Place the jam, orange juice and zest, and spices in a small pan and slowly heat. Brush the mixture over the gammon, wrap in foil, and roast in a preheated oven at 375°F 2½ hours. Remove the foil from the meat and roast 30 minute longer, basting regularly. Carve into thin slices and serve.

turkey

This low-fat, high-protein poultry has incredible muscle-building benefits.

Scientists have found turkey contains one of the highest concentrations of muscle-building substances called dipeptides. In tests, athletes who regularly ate 5-ounce portions of turkey breast meat showed an increase of 40 percent in muscle concentration, and performance improved greatly, especially for runners, rowers, cyclists, and speed skaters.

Turkey leg meat contains twice as much iron and three times as much zinc as breast meat.

NUTRIENTS

Vitamins B2, B3, B6, B12; iron, phosphorus, selenium, zinc

TURKEY SCHNITZEL

4 x 6-oz. turkey breast halves, flattened
3 tbsp. all-purpose flour
1 extra-large egg, beaten
4oz. cornflakes, finely crushed
green salad, to serve

Coat the turkey pieces lightly in the flour. Dip them in the egg and then coat in the cornflakes. Place on a baking tray and bake in a preheated oven at 350°F 30 to 40 minutes until the juices run clear. Serve with a green salad.

chicken

Rated as a protein powerhouse, chicken is perhaps the most versatile meat of all.

A high intake of saturated fats increases the risk of heart disease and piles on the pounds, significantly slowing an athlete down. While all meat and dairy products contain some saturated fat, chicken is one of the leanest, most health-enhancing choices.

ENHANCES PERFORMANCE

Chicken provides a good deal of protein to build and repair muscles and an impressive list of minerals, including magnesium to help reduce the risk of cramps during exercise,

NUTRIENTS

Vitamins A, B2, B3, B6, B12, K; iron, phosphorus, potassium, magnesium, selenium, sodium, zinc

CHICKEN FACTS

*A chicken breast with the skin on contains almost twice as much saturated fat as a skinned chicken breast.

*The white breast meat of chicken contains less fat and fewer calories than the dark meat (wings and legs).

*Chicken is cooked when it's opaque and there's no trace of pink at the bone, and the juices run clear.

* Buying a whole chicken works out cheaper than buying pieces, with the added bonus of having the bones left over to use in soups and stock pots.

BALSAMIC CHICKEN DRUMSTICKS

6 tbsp. balsamic vinegar
2 tbsp. sunflower oil
1 tsp. Dijon mustard
1 tsp. clear honey
½ tsp. salt
1 tsp. freshly ground
　black pepper
8 large chicken drumsticks

In a bowl, mix the vinegar, oil, mustard, honey, and salt and season with pepper. Coat the drumsticks and chill in a shallow baking dish 2 hours. Broil 15 to 20 minutes, turning every 5 minutes until the juices run clear, then serve.

and potassium to balance the fluid levels in the body, as well as selenium and zinc to bolster immunity. Zinc is also known to have energy-boosting properties.

LIFTS MOOD

Chicken is an excellent source of tryptophan, an essential amino acid that helps control the brain's serotonin levels, which are linked to appetite and mood. The B-complex vitamins found in this meat also help to regulate the metabolism.

A 2- to 3-pound chicken can be frozen whole for up to 8 months and takes 10 to 12 hours to thaw.

THAI CHICKEN

1 tsp. ground chilli
1-in. piece ginger root,
    peeled and grated
juice and zest of 1 lime
4 boneless chicken breasts,
    cut into strips
1½ cups coconut milk
1½ cups chicken stock
rice, to serve

In a bowl, mix the chilli, ginger, and lime juice and zest. Place the chicken in a shallow dish, pour over the mixture, cover and chill 1 hour. Bring the coconut milk and stock to a boil in a pan. Reduce the heat, add the chicken, and simmer 15 minutes. Serve with rice.

duck

NUTRIENTS
Vitamins B1, B2, B3, B6, B12; copper, iron, phosphorus, selenium, zinc

Eating roasted or stir-fried duck is an energy-rich way for athletes to hit their daily protein target.

Duck is a good source of protein and iron, both needed to repair tissue and build new cells. It is high in B-vitamins, which combat fatigue and regulate metabolism. Although duck has a reputation as a fat-laden meat, the saturated fat content is five times lower when all the skin is removed. In fact, a skinless duck breast is leaner than a skinless chicken breast.

DUCK STIR-FRY

1 red onion, finely chopped
1 tbsp. sesame oil
2 tbsp. soy sauce
4 Mallard duck breasts, skinned and cut into strips
2 carrots, cut into batons
14 oz. mung bean sprouts
juice and zest of 1 orange
noodles, to serve

In a wok, fry the onion in the oil and soy sauce. Add the duck pieces and fry 5 minutes. Add the bean sprouts and orange juice and zest. Cook 1 minute longer. Serve with noodles.

Game farms will supply Barbary, Mallard and other wild duck meat.

rabbit

A rabbit's strong flavor is an acquired taste for some, but its meat helps revive get-up-and-go.

Like other types of game, rabbits get plenty of exercise so their meat is leaner and lower in fat and calories than beef, lamb, and pork, although equal in the protein stakes. Rabbit meat also contains iron and many of the B-vitamin complex, which all perform useful individual functions in the body, but work best together to ward off general tiredness and lethargy and, thus, boost energy levels for exercise.

NUTRIENTS
Vitamins B1, B2, B3, B6, B12; iron, phosphorus, zinc

RABBIT CASSEROLE

1 rabbit, skinned, boned,
 and chopped into chunks
1 tbsp. all-purpose flour
1 tbsp. vegetable oil
2 onions, chopped
7oz. mushrooms, sliced
a handful rosemary, chopped
½ cup chicken stock
½ cup dry white wine
mashed potatoes, to serve

Coat the rabbit chunks in the flour and, in a Dutch oven, lightly fry in the oil. Add the remaining ingredients and bring to a boil. Cover and bake in a preheated oven at 350°F 2 to 2½ hours until the rabbit is tender. Serve with mashed potatoes.

milk

NUTRIENTS
Vitamins A, B2, B12, D, E, K; calcium, iodine, phosphorus, potassium; omega-3 essential fatty acids

Organic milk contains 70 percent more omega-3 fatty acids than non-organic milk.

Known primarily as a bedtime sleep-inducer, a milky drink makes the perfect sports drink, too.

Milk contains many nutrients, including calcium to strengthen bones, vitamin E to boost immunity, and potassium to protect the heart. Studies show drinking chocolate milk improves endurance more than conventional carbohydrate-only sports drinks, because it contains the ideal ratio of carbohydrates to protein to help refuel tired muscles. Try a homemade milkshake, a smoothie, or a cup of cocoa within two hours of exercise. The body converts these post-exercise calories into glycogen to deliver carbohydrate straight to fuel-depleted muscles.

BEDTIME MILK *serves 2*

2 cups milk
a tiny pinch saffron
2 tbsp. clear honey
1 tsp. grated nutmeg
½ tsp. cinnamon

Gently heat the milk, saffron and honey in a pan, stirring until the honey is dissolved. Pour into cups, sprinkle with the spices, and serve.

yogurt

A brilliant bone-protector, yogurt can be useful for athletes who are unable to tolerate lactose.

Yogurt has a high calcium content, as well as traces of vitamin D, which help the body to absorb calcium and other bone-building minerals, such as magnesium and phosphorus. Eating it regularly reduces the risk of developing osteoporosis, the bone-thinning condition. Even people who can't digest dairy products because their body doesn't produce an enzyme called lactase, can usually eat yogurt because the live cultures in yogurt produce their own lactase.

NUTRIENTS
Vitamins A, B2, B3, B5, B12, C, D, folate; calcium, iodine, iron, magnesium, phosphorus, potassium, selenium, zinc

HEALTHY COLESLAW

4 tbsp. plain yogurt
2 tsp. Dijon mustard
2 tsp. lemon juice
1 small white cabbage, shredded
4 carrots, peeled and grated
1 red onion, thinly sliced

Whisk together the yogurt, mustard, and lemon juice in a bowl. Toss in the cabbage, carrots, and red onion, mixing well. Serve as a side dish.

cheese

NUTRIENTS
Vitamins A, B2, B12; calcium, iodine, phosphorus, selenium

Eating cheese tops up the body's levels of calcium and protein—nutrients crucial for regular exercisers.

Weight-bearing exercise builds strong bones, but it puts them under pressure, increasing the body's need for calcium, which builds bone density. This means cheese makes an ideal snack for athletes or sports players, who also lose calcium in perspiration. In fact, thirty minutes of sweat-inducing exercise increases calcium requirement. Cheese can get a bad press for its high saturated fat content, but studies show eating it after a meal actually boosts the body's ability to burn fat.

REALLY CHEESY SAUCE

¼ cup (½ stick) butter
2 tbsp. all-purpose flour
2 cups 2% milk
¾ cup blue cheese, crumbled
½ cup grated Parmesan cheese
½ tsp. mustard
a pinch cayenne pepper
½ tsp. grated nutmeg
chicken, to serve
wholewheat pasta, to serve

In a pan, melt the butter. Add the flour and slowly stir in the milk. Bring to a boil, then remove from the heat. Stir in the blue cheese, Parmesan, mustard, cayenne pepper, and nutmeg. Serve the sauce over chicken or wholewheat pasta.

Avoid eating foods high in iron at the same time as calcium-rich foods—iron inhibits calcium absorption.

egg

The perfect complete protein, eggs contain all the essential amino acids needed by athletes.

Eggs are an excellent source of B-vitamins, zinc, iron, and phospholipids—fats required for cell membranes and a healthy brain. They're one of the few nonmeat sources of vitamins A, B12, and D, which we need for healthy bones. Eggs are also rich in vitamin K, which helps heal bruises and other minor sports injuries by making sure blood is able to clot normally.

NUTRIENTS

Vitamins A, B2, B3, B5, B6, B12, D, E, folate; calcium, chromium, copper, iodine, iron, magnesium, manganese, phosphorus, potassium, selenium, sodium, zinc; omega-3 essential fatty acids

SMOKED SALMON OMELET

4 large eggs
1oz. smoked salmon, chopped
1 tbsp. olive oil
wholewheat bread, to serve
green salad, to serve

Beat the eggs and mix in the salmon. Heat the oil in a skillet and pour in the egg mixture. Cook the omelet 2 minutes until it is set at the edges, then use a spatula to flip the omelet and cook 30 seconds longer. Serve with wholewheat bread and a green salad.

walnut

The only nut-source of omega-3 essential fatty acid, walnuts make an ideal daily snack for non-fish-eating athletes.

Like all nuts, walnuts are rich in anti-inflammatory, heart-healthy monounsaturated fats, which are important as a concentrated source of energy for anyone who's physically active. Unlike other nuts, walnuts also contain alpha-linoleic acid, an omega-3 essential fatty acid crucial for well-oiled joints and positive mood. Studies show that eating just 1oz of walnuts a day can boost heart-health.

NUTRIENTS

Vitamins B1, B2, B3, B5, B6, E; calcium, copper, iodine, iron, magnesium, manganese, phosphorus, potassium, selenium, zinc; omega-3 essential fatty acids

VEGETARIAN WALNUT BURGERS

1⅓ cups shelled walnuts
4 slices of wholewheat bread, toasted
1 red onion, finely chopped
2 eggs, beaten
2oz. Gorgonzola, crumbled
a handful chives

Grind the walnuts in a food processor. Add the bread and process again. Add the remaining ingredients and process to form a firm mixture. Shape into ½-in. patties. Bake in a preheated oven at 375°F 25–30 minutes until crisp, then serve.

almond

Nibbling on almonds provides nutrients and energy for people who work out, with less risk of piling on unwanted pounds.

With more dietary fiber, calcium, and vitamin E than any other nut, plus protein and heart-friendly monounsaturated fat, almonds are a nutritional powerhouse. It's thought that almonds help the body to burn fat more efficiently, as researchers found that of two groups of people on low-calorie diets, those who ate almonds daily lost 50 percent more fat. This makes the nuts useful for anyone trying to shed fat and build muscle.

70 percent of the fat in almonds is the artery-clearing monounsaturated variety.

NUTRIENTS

Vitamins B1, B2, B3, B5, B6, E, folate; calcium, copper, iodine, iron, magnesium, manganese, phosphorus, potassium, selenium, zinc; omega-6 essential fatty acids

ALMOND MACAROONS
makes 20

2 extra-large egg whites
1½ cups finely ground
    almonds
⅓ cup sugar
1 tsp. almond extract
a pinch salt

In a bowl, beat the egg whites until stiff. Fold in the ground almonds, then gradually fold in the sugar and almond extract. Roll the mixture into small balls and flatten each ball on an oiled cookie tray. Bake in a preheated oven at 350°F 25 minutes, until golden.

hazelnut

A popular ingredient in rich chocolates, hazelnuts also make a scrumptious and nutritious snack in their own right.

Containing plenty of fiber, vitamins, minerals, and protein, raw hazelnuts are a nutrient-dense snack choice. They are particularly rich in omega-9 fatty acid, a monounsaturated fat also known as oleic acid, which boosts the immune system. This helps the body ward off performance-impairing coughs and colds, and is especially important for anyone who regularly trains outdoors near pollution-causing traffic.

HAZELNUT SHORTBREAD

½ cup (1 stick) butter
⅓ cup sugar
1 extra-large egg, beaten
2 tsp. coffee granules, dissolved in 2 tbsp. boiling water
1¾ cups all-purpose flour, sifted
½ cup ground hazelnuts
½ cup ground almonds

In a bowl, beat the butter and sugar until creamy, then fold in the egg and coffee. Stir in the flour and nuts, then roll out the dough between two sheets of baking paper and chill overnight. Cut into squares and bake on a tray in a preheated oven at 300°F 20 to 25 minutes until golden brown.

Hazelnuts contain cardio-protective arginine, an amino acid that relaxes blood vessels.

pine nut

Pine nuts are perfect with pasta, in stir-fries or salads, or as an energy-boosting snack.

The small edible seeds of the pine tree, pine nuts are lower in fat content than most other nuts, which means they're a brilliant choice for weight-conscious athletes who need to get plenty of muscle-building protein and joint-friendly essential fats in their diet without overloading on calories. High in immunity-boosting antioxidant vitamin E, pine nuts are also nature's only source of pinoleic acid, a substance found to stimulate the hormones that help to diminish appetite.

NUTRIENTS
Vitamins B1, B2, B3, E; copper, iron, magnesium, manganese, zinc; omega-6 essential fatty acids

GOAT CHEESE PESTO

⅔ cup pine nuts
4oz. mild, soft goat cheese
¼ cup grated Parmesan
2oz. fresh basil
juice of 1 lemon
2 garlic cloves, crushed
⅓ cup sun-dried tomatoes
pasta, to serve

Blend all the ingredients in a food processor until smooth. Serve with pasta.

063

pistachio

These easy-to-open, pale green nuts are heart-smart and help to maintain good eyesight.

Cardiovascular fitness is central to any exercise regime and studies show eating 1 ounce of monounsaturated fat-loaded pistachios a day decreases the incidence of heart disease between 20 to 60 percent.

STRENGTHENS BONES

Pistachios are a good choice because they're also packed with the minerals essential for optimum fitness. Calcium keeps the bones strong; copper increases energy, protects joints, and helps the body to utilize iron; magnesium combats muscle fatigue; and zinc speeds up recovery from muscular injuries.

NUTRIENTS
Vitamins B1, B3, E; calcium, copper, magnesium, manganese, potassium, zinc; omega-6 essential fatty acids

PISTACHIO FACTS
*The pistachio is a member of the cashew family.

*Pistachio trees are planted in orchards, and take up to ten years to produce a significant amount of nuts.

*One serving of pistachios (about 45 kernels) provides as much potassium as half a banana.

*Pistachios contain seven amino acids.

PISTACHIO AND MANGO LASSI *serves 1*

3 tbsp. plain yogurt
⅓ cup pistachios, shelled
½ mango, peeled
2 tsp. sugar

Blend the yogurt, nuts, mango, and sugar with ½ cup water in a food processor. Serve over ice.

PROTECTS EYESIGHT

Pistachios are also the only nuts that contain high levels of lutein and zeaxanthin, antioxidants needed to maintain eye health, which is particularly important in racket and team sports where good hand–eye and foot–eye coordination is a key skill.

PISTACHIO COUSCOUS

1 cup couscous
4 cardamom pods, crushed
1 tsp. salt
a handful mint
⅔ cup pistachios, shelled
½ tsp. grated nutmeg

Bring 1¾ cups water to a boil in a large pan. Reduce the heat, add the couscous, cardamom pods, salt, and mint, and simmer 10 minutes. Remove from the heat. Mix in the pistachios with a fork, sprinkle with the nutmeg, and serve.

Pistachios are known as the "smiling nut" in Iran and the "happy nut" in China.

cashew

Cashew nuts make a handy, nutrient-loaded snack when you've worked up an appetite exercising.

NUTRIENTS
Vitamins B2, B3, B5, B6, folate; copper, iodine, iron, magnesium, manganese, phosphorus, potassium, selenium, zinc

Cashews are rich in many of the minerals that active people need. For example, 30 cashews provides one-fifth of most women's recommended daily iron intake, while 20 nuts provide more than one-tenth of most men's daily zinc requirement. The phosphorus in the nuts works with the calcium to form and maintain strong bones, while the copper has healing properties, and can help to rid the body of infections.

CASHEW NUT DIP

⅔ cup cashews
1 tbsp. crunchy peanut butter
3 garlic cloves, crushed
3 tbsp. olive oil
juice of 1 lemon
scant ½ cup tahini
a pinch paprika
pita bread, to serve

Blend all the ingredients in a food processor until smooth. Serve with pita bread.

Cashews grow on an edible, fruitlike structure known as the "cashew apple."

Brazil nut

These mineral-rich marvels are great for perking up anyone whose fitness levels are flagging.

Brazil nuts are renowned for their high selenium content, a nutrient with potent antioxidant properties that reduces the risk of heart disease and cancer. Selenium also lifts a low mood, helping to relieve depression, anxiety, and fatigue. Four Brazil nuts provide the recommended daily amount of selenium for most adults. They are also rich in magnesium, which is important for the formation of protein and boosting energy levels.

NUTRIENTS

Vitamins B1, E; calcium, copper, iron, magnesium, manganese, phosphorus, selenium, zinc; omega-3 and -6 essential fatty acids

CHOCOLATE-DIPPED BRAZIL NUTS

2oz. dark chocolate
1 tbsp. crystalized ginger, finely chopped
⅔ cup Brazil nuts, shelled

Line a baking tray with waxed paper. Break the chocolate into pieces, put it in a heatproof bowl and slowly melt over a pan of boiling water. Stir in the ginger and coat the nuts in the mixture. Place the nuts on the tray, making sure they don't touch. Refrigerate until the chocolate sets, then serve.

chestnut

Chestnuts have the lowest fat and the highest carbohydrate content of all nuts, as well as a pleasantly sweet flavor.

The low-fat, high-carbohydrate content of chestnuts is a dream combination for anyone watching their calorie intake and wishing to boost their energy levels before a work-out. Unlike other tree nuts, the insides of chestnuts are not hard, but soft and fleshy, and cannot be eaten raw as they contain very high levels of tannic acids, which can cause digestive discomfort. This means they need to be boiled or roasted before eating.

CHESTNUT AND LIMA BEAN SOUP

14oz. chestnuts, cooked and peeled
14oz. canned lima beans, drained and rinsed
3 shallots, chopped
1 large carrot, chopped
2 cups vegetable stock
bread, to serve

Place all the ingredients in a pan, cover and bring to the boil. Reduce the heat and simmer gently 20 minutes. Puree until smooth. Serve with bread.

Before roasting chestnuts, slit the shells to let steam escape and prevent the nuts from bursting.

coconut

Easily digested and metabolized by the body, coconut is a great preexercise energy source.

Although coconut is high in saturated fats known as medium-chain fatty acids (MCFAs), these don't pose the same negative health risk as other saturated fats. This is because the body uses them as instant energy rather than storing them as fat. The coconut water—the liquid inside the coconut—is known to be one of the most balanced natural electrolyte sources, making it a wonderfully rehydrating drink after intensive exercise.

NUTRIENTS

Vitamins B1, B2, B3, B5, B6, C, E, folate; calcium, copper, iodine, iron, magnesium, manganese, phosphorus, potassium, selenium, zinc

COCONUT RICE

heaped ½ cup brown rice
1 onion, chopped
2 tbsp. coconut oil
1 tbsp. ground coriander
1 tbsp. ground cumin
2 beef tomatoes, chopped
3 tbsp. finely shredded
    coconut

Place the rice and 1¾ cups of water in a pan and bring to a boil. Simmer 45 minutes. In another pan, fry the onion in the oil and spices 3 minutes. Add the tomato and coconut, and simmer 10 minutes longer. Mix well with the rice. Serve as a side dish.

pumpkin seed

NUTRIENTS

Vitamins B2, B3, B5, E, K, beta-carotene; calcium, copper, iron, magnesium, manganese, phosphorus, potassium, zinc; omega-3 and -6 essential fatty acids

Boasting the highest iron content in the seed world, pumpkin seeds make a very nutritious nibble.

The easily absorbed iron in pumpkin seeds encourages the formation of red blood cells and helps pump oxygen around the body efficiently, making fatigue and low energy levels during exercise less likely. These seeds are rich in omega-3 oils, which are anti-inflammatory and protect joints from damage during high-impact activities. They also promote the healing of sports-related injuries.

PUMPKIN SEED GRANOLA

2 tbsp. coconut oil
2 tbsp. maple syrup
1 cup rolled oats
4 tbsp. pumpkin seeds
1 tbsp. sesame seeds
2 tbsp. finely ground almonds
1 tbsp. desiccated coconut
plain yogurt, to serve

In a pan, fry the oil, syrup, and oats over a low heat 3 minutes. Mix in the seeds, almonds, and coconut and spread out over a baking tray. Bake at 300°F 25 minutes. Allow to cool and serve with plain yogurt.

Pumpkin seeds are often recommended for men as a remedy for prostate enlargement.

flaxseed

Thanks to their essential fatty acids, flaxseeds are hailed as "superseeds" across the globe.

Flaxseeds are top of the nutrition league when it comes to heart-healthy and joint-friendly omega-3 content. They provide calcium for bone strength and magnesium to help ward off muscle cramps and release energy. As flaxseeds and their oils are easily oxidized, causing them to go rancid, keep them in dark bottles or tubs with sealed lids, and store them in the refrigerator for no longer than a year.

NUTRIENTS
Calcium, magnesium, zinc; omega-3 essential fatty acids

FLAXSEED MUFFINS
makes 12

½ cup golden flaxseeds, ground
1¼ cups wholewheat flour
1 tbsp. baking powder
2 tsp. ground allspice
1 cup light brown sugar
1 egg, beaten
1 cup plus 2 tbsp. milk

Mix the seeds, flour, baking powder, allspice and sugar in a bowl. Add the egg and milk. Spoon the batter into 12 paper cases in a muffin pan. Bake in a preheated oven at 350°F 25 minutes. Cool on a wire rack.

070

sesame seed

NUTRIENTS
Vitamins B1, B2, B3, B5, B6,
E, beta-carotene; calcium,
copper, iodine, iron, magnesium,
manganese, phosphorus,
potassium, zinc; omega-6 essential
fatty acids

A fantastic source of calcium, sesame seeds are brilliant nondairy bone-builders.

These tiny seeds are often used to make tahini or sesame paste, or simply scattered over stir-fries, salads, and pasta. They are packed with calcium, containing more of this important mineral than most foods, including whole milk. Sesame seeds are also a great source of vitamin-B complex, which, together with the omega-6 essential fatty acids, help to keep the heart healthy and release energy to enhance stamina and fight fatigue.

NUTTY BANANA PUDDING

heaped 1 cup roasted peanuts
¼ cup (½ stick) butter
2 tbsp. maple syrup
1 tbsp. tahini
4 bananas, peeled
½ cup sesame seeds

Grind the peanuts in a blender. In a pan, gently melt the butter and stir in the maple syrup, tahini, and ground peanuts. Coat each banana carefully with the mixture and a sprinkling of sesame seeds. Allow to cool and serve.

In ancient India, sesame seeds were a symbol of immortality.

sunflower seed

Eating sunflower seeds helps to maintain a healthy heart, which is key to reaching optimum fitness.

Sunflower seeds are an excellent source of vitamin E, the body's primary fat-soluble antioxidant that does the important job of neutralizing harmful free radicals, promoting healthy blood flow, and regulating the heartbeat. These seeds also contain lots of magnesium, crucial for healthy bones and muscles. Other potent minerals found in sunflower seeds include selenium and zinc, which protect from disease.

NUTRIENTS
Vitamins B1, B2, B5, E, folate; calcium, copper, iron, magnesium, manganese, phosphorus, selenium, zinc; omega-6 essential fatty acids

TABBOULEH WITH SUNFLOWER SEEDS

1 cup bulgur wheat
1¾ cups hot vegetable stock
4 tbsp. sunflower seeds
2 tbsp. flaxseeds
1 red onion, finely chopped
½ cucumber, diced
3 tomatoes, diced
a handful parsley, chopped
a handful mint, chopped

In a bowl, mix the bulgur wheat and stock, cover, and leave 30 minutes. Mix in the remaining ingredients with a fork and serve.

cornmeal

Cornmeal and cornstarch are nutritious, gluten-free options for anyone who can't tolerate wheat.

Ground into meal or flour, corn is a useful kitchen staple for making bread and tortillas and for thickening sauces and puddings. It's a complex carbohydrate, which means it keeps blood sugar stable for longer during exercise. Also, research has found switching from white flour to lower-fat wholegrain corn helps prevent anemia, because it increases the body's ability to absorb iron by up to 50 percent.

NUTRIENTS
Vitamins B3, B5, C, folate; calcium, magnesium, potassium, zinc

CORN CRISPBREAD

⅔ cup cornstarch
¾ cup brown rice flour
¼ cup milk
½ tsp. salt

In a bowl, mix all the ingredients with to make a soft dough. On a floured surface, roll out to a thickness of ¼-in, and cut into rectangles. Place on a greased baking sheet and bake in a preheated oven at 400°F 8 to 10 minutes until golden. Cool on a wire rack.

Yellow cornmeal is also known as maize and polenta.

barley

Barley is the perfect prerace fuel-provider for long-distance runners, cyclists, and swimmers.

This glutinous grain has a chewy texture similar to pasta and is an excellent source of complex carbohydrate, which means it balances blood-sugar levels and releases energy slowly over time to give endurance athletes more strength and stamina. It's also a great source of B-vitamins, which also help boost energy. All types of barley are nutrient-rich, but pot barley retains much more fiber than pearl barley. Soak barley overnight in cold water before adding to warming soups or stews.

NUTRIENTS
Vitamins B1, B2, B3, B5, B6, B9, B12, folate; calcium, iron, magnesium, manganese, phosphorus, potassium, selenium, zinc

BAKED BARLEY

½ cup pearl barley
1 onion, finely chopped
1 tbsp. olive oil
1 tbsp. tomato paste
a handful basil leaves
a handful thyme
juice of ½ lemon

Bring 1½ cups water to a boil in a Dutch oven. Gradually stir in all the ingredients. Cover and bake in a preheated oven at 375°F 40 minutes. Fluff with a fork and serve.

millet

This king of the complex carbohydrates helps to keep the body strong for optimum fitness.

Easy to digest, millet is high in silica, needed for healthy tendons and bones. This small, round grain is also protein-rich, containing all the eight essential amino acids that aid recovery of sports-related injuries. Unlike most grains, millet is alkaline-forming, so it might help neutralize acidic conditions that affect the joints, such as arthritis. It's also high in B-vitamins, which are known to boost energy and combat stress. Millet is loaded with the health-enhancing minerals calcium and magnesium, which are essential for building strong bones.

NUTRIENTS
Vitamins B1, B2, B3, B5, B6, E, K, folate; calcium, copper, iron, magnesium, manganese, phosphorus, potassium, selenium, silica, zinc

MILLET PORRIDGE

1 cup 2% milk
½ cup millet
½ cup raisins
2 tsp. honey
a pinch nutmeg

Pour the milk and ½ cup water into a pan and add the millet. Bring to a boil and simmer 15 minutes, stirring all the time. Add the raisins and honey. Sprinkle over the nutmeg and serve.

rye

A high-fiber low-GI grain, rye makes a great pre-workout snack, as it staves off hunger pangs and helps to prevent fluid retention.

With more insoluble fiber and less gluten than wheat, rye is a wholegrain cereal that's commonly milled into flour and made into stamina-building bread. This is ideal for athletes, as it releases energy slowly, preventing hunger pangs and energy dips. Rye is rich in plant lignans, which help reduce blood viscosity, and sucrose and fructooligosaccharide, which have prebiotic properties that help prevent bloating.

NUTRIENTS
Vitamins B1, B2, B3, B5, B6, B9, B12, E; calcium, iron, magnesium, manganese, phosphorus, potassium, selenium, zinc

RYE BREAD

1 cup plus 2 tbsp.
  dark rye flour
2¾ cups all-purpose flour
2 tsp. active dry yeast
½ cup dark brown sugar
2 tsp. salt
1 egg, beaten
1 tbsp. vegetable oil

Mix the flours, yeast, sugar, and salt in a bowl. Add the egg, oil, and 1 cup warm water and knead 10 minutes into a dough. Cover and leave for 1 hour or until double in size. Knead into a ball and leave on an oiled baking sheet 30 minutes. Bake in a preheated oven at 400°F 30 to 35 minutes.

Rye bread, such as pumpernickel, is widely eaten across Central and Eastern Europe.

076

buckwheat

NUTRIENTS
Vitamins B1, B2, B3, B5, B6, E, K, folate; calcium, copper, iron, magnesium, manganese, phosphorus, potassium, selenium, zinc

Eating this wholesome grain can reduce the risk of broken veins and chilblains while training outdoors in winter.

Buckwheat is extremely rich in a natural chemical called rutin, which keeps the inner lining of blood vessels clear and helps prevent chilblains and broken veins. For anyone with a wheat or gluten allergy, soba noodles, found in supermarkets and Asian groceries, are often made with 100 percent gluten-free buckwheat. These noodles have an earthy, grainlike taste and can be used hot or cold in salads and stir-fries.

BUCKWHEAT BLINIS
makes 12 to 14

1 cup milk
1 egg
1 tsp. olive oil, plus
   extra for frying
½ cup buckwheat flour
½ cup wholewheat flour
a pinch salt

In a food processor, blend the milk, egg, and oil together. Add the flours and salt, and blend until smooth. Heat a little oil in a nonstick pan and fry 1 tablespoon of batter to make each blini, cooking 2 minutes on each side, then serve.

amaranth

This tiny, nutritious wholegrain is a fantastic source of complete protein and complex carbohydrates.

Researchers found that athletes who ate a low-GI wholegrain, such as amaranth, before exercise were able to keep going considerably longer than those who ate a high-GI, white-flour-based food. It's also been found that low-GI grains can help the body to burn more fat during exercise. Amaranth contains more iron and calcium than most other grains, helping to boost overall energy levels and bone strength.

NUTRIENTS
Vitamins B1, B2, B3, B5, B6, C, E, folate; calcium, copper, iron, magnesium, phosphorus, potassium, zinc

AMARANTH PUDDING

1 cup amaranth
1 cup milk
½ cup finely ground almonds
¼ cup sugar
1 tbsp. cocoa powder
2oz. dark chocolate

Mix the amaranth, milk, almonds, sugar, and cocoa in a large pan. Cover and bring to a boil. Reduce the heat and simmer 15 minutes. Pour into pudding bowls, grate the chocolate over, and serve.

Amaranth was a staple grain for the Aztec civilization of central Mexico.

oats

Usually eaten as an energy-packed breakfast and in oatmeal cookies and cereal bars, oats regularly feature in line-ups of the "top-ten" superfoods.

NUTRIENTS

Vitamins B1, B2, B3, B5, B6, E, K, folate; calcium, copper, iron, magnesium, manganese, phosphorus, potassium, selenium, silica, zinc

Oats release their energy very slowly and can keep an athlete going for hours, because they are an excellent source of wholegrain complex carbohydrates. They also contain more protein than most other grains and are bursting with soluble fiber, which helps eliminate cholesterol from the body. Whole oats (also known as groats) consist of the whole grain with the hull removed. Rolled oats are whole oats that have been flattened between rollers.

OATY BREAKFAST PANCAKES

2 extra-large eggs
¼ cup (½ stick) butter
1 tbsp. light brown sugar
1 tsp. cinnamon
1¼ cups rolled oats
1 tbsp. baking powder
1 tbsp. vegetable oil

Blend the eggs, butter, sugar, and cinnamon in a food processor. Stir in the oats and baking powder. Fry tablespoons of the batter in the oil and cook 1 to 2 minutes on each side and serve.

wheat

Wheat often gets a bad press, but it can be a top source of carbohydrate for endurance athletes.

A reduction in the body's carbohydrate stores is one of the major causes of fatigue during prolonged exercise. White flour doesn't provide many nutrients, but other wheat sources are a nutritious way to top up carbohydrate levels. Have wholegrain pasta as a preexercise meal, beef up a smoothie with wheat germ (the seed found inside the wheat grain) or use bulgur wheat (a mineral-rich cracked wheat grain), in place of white rice.

NUTRIENTS

Vitamins B1, B2, B3, E, folate; copper, iron, magnesium, manganese, phosphorus, zinc

Wheat is the world's most widely cultivated plant, grown on every continent except Antarctica.

CREAMY GREEN SPAGHETTI

10oz. wholewheat spaghetti
1 cup coarse fresh
   wholewheat breadcrumbs
zest of 1 lime
1 garlic clove, crushed
8oz. watercress
1 cup single cream
½ tsp. grated nutmeg

Cook the spaghetti in boiling, salted water 12 minutes. In a bowl mix together the breadcrumbs, lime zest, and garlic, spread on a baking sheet and broil 3 to 4 minutes. Drain the spaghetti and stir in the breadcrumbs, watercress, and cream. Sprinkle with the nutmeg and serve immediately.

quinoa

Pronounced "keen-waa," quinoa is one of the best sources of protein in the plant kingdom.

NUTRIENTS
Vitamins B1, B2, B3, B5, B6, E, folate; calcium, copper, iron, magnesium, manganese, phosphorus, potassium, zinc

Strictly speaking, quinoa is a seed, not a grain. Low in fat, it's full of slow-release carbohydrates, which balance blood sugar.

BUILDS STRENGTH

Containing all eight essential amino acids, quinoa is an exceptionally rich source of protein, making it a useful addition

> Quinoa is loaded with lysine, an amino acid that is essential for tissue growth and repair.

QUINOA-STUFFED PEPPERS

1¼ cups quinoa
1 onion, chopped
2 garlic cloves, crushed
4oz. mushrooms, chopped
1 tbsp. olive oil
4 red bell peppers
green salad, to serve

In a large pan, bring 2 cups water to a boil. Stir in the quinoa and simmer 15 minutes. In another pan, cook the onion, garlic, and mushrooms in the oil until soft. Add the cooked quinoa and mix well. Cut the tops off the peppers and remove the cores and seeds. Fill each pepper with the quinoa mixture, replace the tops, and place them in a baking dish. Bake in a preheated oven at 375°F 45 minutes. Serve with a green salad.

to the diet of regular exercisers and serious athletes, who need more protein than inactive people. (An insufficient intake delays the body's recovery after training and slows the development of muscle and stamina.)

BOOSTS ENERGYY

A serving of quinoa provides nearly the entire spectrum of B-vitamins, needed to boost energy and combat stress as well as lots of vitamin E, a key component in skin health and the body's healing process. Quinoa is also rich in calcium and magnesium, essential for healthy bones, iron to help prevent fatigue, and zinc to enhance the immune system.

QUINOA FACTS

*Quinoa was once called "the gold of the Incas," who recognized its value in increasing the stamina of their warriors.

*When quinoa is cooked, the grains become translucent and the white germ partially detaches itself, appearing like a white-spiraled tail.

*For a nuttier flavor, dry roast quinoa before cooking in a heavy-bottomed pan over medium-low heat, stirring constantly 5 minutes.

*The leaves of the quinoa plant are edible, with a taste similar to its green-leafed relatives, spinach and chard.

spelt

Containing more nutrients than its better-known distant cousin, wheat, this ancient grain is now regaining popularity.

Used to make bread and pasta, spelt is exceptionally high in manganese. In fact, a 4-ounce serving provides two-thirds of the recommended daily intake for most adults of this mineral, which is invaluable for athletes as it is vital for many bodily functions, including bone and connective tissue formation, thyroid function, calcium absorption, blood-sugar regulation, and fat and carbohydrate metabolism. Spelt is also an important source of zinc and selenium, which boost immunity.

NUTRIENTS

Vitamins A, B1, B2, B3, B6, E, folate; calcium, copper, magnesium, manganese, phosphorus, potassium, selenium, zinc

SPELT CRACKERS WITH TRICOLORE SALAD

2 avocados, peeled and pitted
juice of ½ lemon
8 spelt crackers
4 tomatoes, thinly sliced
4oz. mozzarella,
    finely sliced
salt
freshly ground black pepper

In a bowl, mash the avocados with the lemon juice and season with salt and pepper. Spread over the crackers and top with a layer of tomato and mozzarella slices, then serve.

triticale

A nutritious alternative to wheat, triticale is a great source of carbohydrate, boosting stamina during matches and workouts.

Triticale is a hybrid of wheat and rye that was first bred in Sweden and Scotland in the late-nineteenth century. Today, cracked triticale can be used in the same way as cracked wheat, and triticale flakes make a great substitute for oat flakes. It is high in folate, which protects against heart disease, as well as calcium and magnesium, crucial for healthy bones.

The word "triticale" is an amalgamation of the Latin words *triticum* (wheat) and *secale* (rye).

NUTRIENTS
Vitamins B1, folate; calcium, iron, magnesium

MUSHROOM BAKE

1 onion, finely chopped
1lb. 2oz. mushrooms, halved
1 tbsp. olive oil
1 cup triticale flour
1 tbsp. tomato paste
a handful oregano
salad, to serve

In a pan, fry the onion and mushrooms in the oil. In a bowl, mix the flour and tomato paste with ¼ cup water to form a smooth paste. Add the oregano and mix all the ingredients together. Transfer to a lightly greased baking dish, cover, and bake in a preheated oven at 325°F 20 minutes. Serve with salad.

brown rice

With its nutty flavor, brown rice is a heart-warming grain that tastes good hot or cold.

Rice is one of the most easily digested grains, which is why rice cereal is often recommended as a baby's first solid. Retaining both the bran and germ of the rice kernel, brown rice is a source of protein, carbohydrates, and fiber. Brown basmati rice contains more amylose than other types of rice, which means it is less rapidly absorbed into the body, providing a steady stream of energy for exercisers, rather than a spike followed by a slump.

NUTRIENTS
Vitamins B1, B3, B5, B6, E, K, folate; calcium, copper, iodine, iron, magnesium, manganese, phosphorus, potassium, selenium, zinc

INDIAN WHOLEGRAIN PILAF

1 tsp. ground cumin
1 tsp. ground turmeric
1 tsp. ground coriander
4 cloves
6 cardamom pods, crushed
2 shallots, finely chopped
1 tbsp. butter
2¼ cups long-grain brown rice
vegetable curry, to serve

Fry the spices and shallots in the butter 3 minutes. Stir in the rice 2 minutes, then add 4½ cups water. Bring to a boil, reduce the heat, and simmer, covered, 25 minutes. Serve with curry.

Studies show the oil in whole brown rice lowers blood cholesterol levels.

wild rice

Chewy in texture, wild rice is rich in protein, packed with dietary fiber and low in fat.

Wild rice is not really rice, but a type of grass containing twice the protein of white rice and fewer calories and fat. Nutritionally, it is one of the few grains that also provides the essential fatty acids omega-3 and -6, which are mostly found in oily fish, nuts, and seeds. It's also an ideal preworkout food, as it's an excellent source of the energy-boosting B-vitamins, thiamine (B1), riboflavin (B2), and niacin (B3).

NUTRIENTS
Vitamins B1, B2, B3, E; iodine, phosphorus, potassium, selenium, zinc; omega-3 and -6 essential fatty acids

SALMON AND WILD RICE STEW

2 red onions, finely chopped
1 tbsp. olive oil
½ cup wild rice
3 cups fish stock
½ cup basmati rice
1lb. 2oz. salmon fillets, cut into large pieces
a handful dill, chopped
2 tbsp. crème fraîche

In a pan, fry the onions in the oil until soft, then stir in the wild rice and stock. Bring to a boil and cook 15 minutes. Stir in the basmati rice, cover, reduce the heat, and cook 20 minutes. Add the salmon. Cook 7 minutes. Flake the salmon, stir in the dill and crème fraîche, and serve.

lentil

One of the best foods for endurance sports, lentils also provide a dose of the feel-good factor.

NUTRIENTS
Vitamins B3, B5, B6, B9, folate; calcium, iron, magnesium, manganese, phosphorus, potassium, selenium, zinc

SWEET-AND-SOUR LENTILS

1¼ cups red lentils
2 tbsp. vegetable oil
2 chopped dried red chilies
½ tsp. mustard seeds
2 tbsp. soy sauce
1 tbsp. sugar
¼ cup pineapple juice
1 tbsp. white wine vinegar

Place the lentils in a pan, cover with water, and bring to a boil. Cover, reduce the heat, and simmer 40 minutes, then drain. In another pan, heat the oil and spices 3 minutes. Add the soy sauce, sugar, juice, vinegar, lentils, and ½ cup water. Simmer 10 minutes longer, then serve.

Packed with protein and slow-releasing natural sugars, lentils are great for stabilizing blood-sugar levels and maintaining stamina. In fact, one study found that eating lentils three hours before exercise can help increase endurance significantly more than other carbohydrates. Lentils are also crammed full of folate, an energy-boosting vitamin that plays a key role in the production of serotonin, the neurotransmitter in the brain associated with feeling happy.

Puy lentils are small and sweet, and hold their shape when cooked.

chickpea

Chickpeas are handy hormone balancers for female athletes prone to performance-impairing PMS.

Throughout the Middle East, India, and Latin America, chickpeas are a stomach-filling staple. Rich in plant hormones, isoflavones, which mimic estrogen in the body, chickpeas can help prevent hormone-related conditions, such as premenstrual syndrome and menopausal hot flashes. Their high B-vitamin content also supports the functions of nerves and muscles, while their high carbohydrate content provides energy.

NUTRIENTS
Vitamins B1, B2, B3, B5, B6, E, K, beta-carotene, folate; calcium, copper, iodine, iron, magnesium, manganese, phosphorus, potassium, selenium, zinc

CHICKPEA AND WALNUT SALAD

heaped 1 cup dried chickpeas
10 scallions, chopped
7 oz. watercress
7 oz. arugula leaves
a handful mint
3 tbsp. olive oil
2 tbsp. balsamic vinegar
heaped 1 cup grated Parmesan

Soak the chickpeas overnight, drain, and place in a pan. Cover with water and bring to a boil. Reduce the heat and simmer 2 hours. Once cool, mix well with the scallions, watercress, arugula, mint, oil, and vinegar in a large bowl. Sprinkle with the cheese and serve.

adzuki bean

Reduce pace-slowing water retention by including this tasty little legume on the menu.

NUTRIENTS

Vitamins B1, B3, B5, B6, E, beta-carotene, folate; calcium, copper, iodine, iron, magnesium, manganese, phosphorus, potassium, selenium, zinc

Containing more fiber and protein and less fat than most other beans, adzuki beans are rich in B-vitamins for steady energy production and body tissue repair. They're also high in many minerals needed for optimal fitness: fatigue-fighting iron; potassium, which acts as a natural diuretic by helping the body to eliminate excess fluid; and immunity-boosting minerals zinc, calcium, and magnesium.

ADZUKI BEAN HOT POT

½ cup dried adzuki beans
1 large onion, chopped
3 carrots, peeled and diced
2 parsnips, peeled and diced
2 sweet potatoes, peeled and diced
2 bay leaves
1 tbsp. tomato paste

Soak the beans overnight in cold water. Drain and put in a pan with water to cover. Bring to a boil, reduce the heat and simmer, uncovered, 45 minutes, then drain. Put all the ingredients in a large baking dish and cover with water. Bake in a preheated oven at 375°F 90 minutes, then serve.

In Japan, these small red legumes are known as the "king of beans".

edamame

Snacking on edamame—loaded with protein iron, carbohydrates and fiber—provides athletes with a serious stamina boost.

Edamame, which look like a cross between fava beans and peas, are baby soy beans prepared in the pod. Hailed as the latest superfood, the pods are picked while still young and tender. Very popular in Japan, China and Korea, edamame are high in fiber, bone-friendly protein, and slow-releasing carbohydrates to help prevent mood fluctuations by keeping blood-sugar levels steady.

NUTRIENTS

Vitamins A, C, folate; calcium, iron; omega-3 essential fatty acids

ROASTED EDAMAME BEANS

½ tsp. ground chili
¼ tsp. ground coriander
¼ tsp. ground ginger
¼ tsp. ground cumin
¼ tsp. turmeric
a pinch paprika
2 tsp. sunflower oil
14oz. ready-to-eat
   edamame pods

In a small bowl, mix the spices with the oil. Toss the beans in to coat and place on a baking tray. Bake in a preheated oven at 375°F 5 to 10 minutes. Leave to cool. Serve as a snack or a side dish.

peanut

Peanuts and peanut butter are packed with protein and heart-healthy fats—a great source of energy for exercise and sports.

In spite of their name, peanuts aren't a nut, but a legume. They're loaded with protein (20 to 30 percent) to help muscles stay strong and have a low GI score, which means they help keep blood-sugar levels stable.

LOWER CHOLESTEROL

On the heart-health front, peanuts contain vitamin E, the amino acid arginine, and oleic acid (the monounsaturated fat found in olive oil), all of which have been shown to reduce

---

PEANUT SHORTBREAD

1¼ cups roasted peanuts
1 tbsp. chunky peanut butter
½ cup sugar
1 tsp. baking soda
1 tsp. all-purpose flour

Finely grind the peanuts in a blender. In a large bowl, mix all the ingredients well. Press into a small, greased baking pan. Bake at 325°F 25 minutes. Leave to cool, cut into squares, and serve.

high cholesterol levels in the blood and to protect against the formation of plaque in the arteries, which clogs them up.

FIGHT DISEASE

Peanuts also contain thirty times more resveratrol than grapes – resveratrol is one of a class of compounds called phytoalexins, associated with reduced cardiovascular disease.

Peanuts grow underground, which is why they're also referred to as groundnuts.

INDONESIAN-STYLE PEANUT SAUCE

⅔ cup shelled, skinned peanuts
juice and zest of 1 lime
1 cup unsweetened canned coconut milk
1 tbsp. tamarind paste
1 tbsp. curry powder
6 scallions, finely chopped
vegetables, shrimp or chicken, to serve

Blend the peanuts and lime juice in a blender to form a paste. Transfer to a pan and stir in the remaining ingredients and ½ cup water. Cook over low heat 7 minutes. Serve over vegetables, shrimp or chicken.

butter bean

Similar to the lima bean, this soft bean has digestion-friendly fiber and potent detoxifying properties.

Like all beans, butter beans are loaded with fiber, and can be a good source of protein, vital to athletes for bone strength when combined with other vegetable proteins, such as rice or quinoa. Butter beans are especially rich in the trace mineral, molybdenum, which has been shown to help the body detoxify toxic sulfites—a type of preservative linked to headaches and asthmalike symptoms, which is added to processed foods, "deli" salads, baked goods, and wine.

NUTRIENTS

Vitamins B1, B3, B5, folate; copper, iron, magnesium, manganese, molybdenum, phosphorus, potassium, zinc

---

BUTTER BEAN AND BROCCOLI SOUP

2 onions, chopped
2 tsp. grated nutmeg
2 tbsp. olive oil
6 cups chicken stock
1lb. canned butter or
   lima beans
3 cups broccoli florets
1 large potato, peeled and
   chopped into 1-in. cubes
bread, to serve

In a pan, gently cook the onions and nutmeg in the oil 5 minutes. Add the stock, beans, broccoli, and potato. Bring to the boil and simmer 15 minutes, or until tender. Puree in a blender and serve with crusty bread.

kidney bean

A Mexican food staple, these versatile beans work well in chilis, salads, dips, and wraps.

A single serving of kidney beans provides lots of protein and a substantial amount of fibre. This is beneficial for regular exercisers who want to lose weight, because fiber curbs hunger for longer, while protein is a wonderful source of energy. Kidney beans are also rich in folate, which helps speed up wound healing—useful for anyone prone to blisters.

NUTRIENTS

Vitamins B1, B6, K, folate; copper, iron, magnesium, manganese, molybdenum, phosphorus, potassium, zinc

MEXICAN BEAN DIP

1¼ cups dried kidney beans
½ onion, finely chopped
½ tsp. ground chilli
1 tbsp. olive oil
2 tbsp. chopped cilantro
2 tbsp. sour cream

Soak the kidney beans in water overnight, then drain. Place in a pan and cover with water. Bring to a boil and boil 10 minutes. Then reduce the heat and simmer 2 hours, or until soft. In another pan, gently fry the onion and chili in the oil 5 minutes. Allow to cool, then puree with the kidney beans, sour cream, and cilantro in a blender and serve.

Kidney beans are highly toxic if consumed raw, so always eat cooked or canned beans.

pinto bean

NUTRIENTS
Vitamin B1, B6, folate; copper, iron, magnesium, manganese, phosphorus, potassium, selenium, zinc

Stay "full of beans" with this excellent low-fat, low-calorie source of protein.

Combine the creamy pink texture of pinto beans with a whole grain, such as brown rice, for a virtually fat-free, high-quality protein meal. Pinto beans are especially rich in the amino acid lysine, which is lacking in most plant proteins. One average serving provides around one quarter of most adults' daily recommended intake of iron, essential for transporting oxygen around the body and keeping up energy levels during exercise.

PINTO BEAN FUDGE

**6oz. dark chocolate
(70 percent cocoa solids)
6 tbsp. butter
¼ cup milk
3oz. drained, canned
pinto beans, mashed
1 tsp. peppermint extract
2lb. powdered sugar**

In a small pan, gently melt the chocolate and butter with the milk. Add the pinto beans and peppermint extract and then gradually add the sugar, stirring continuously to form a thick mixture. Spread the mixture over a greased baking tray, then cover and chill. Once the fudge has set, chop into squares and serve.

Pinto means "painted" in Spanish —uncooked, these beans are beige with reddish brown splashes of color.

soy bean

Soy beans contain more protein than dairy products and have similar bone-protecting properties.

The top-ranking legume on the nutritional scale, soy beans are a source of complete protein, as they contain all eight amino acids. Soy beans are loaded with isoflavones, hormonelike plant chemicals that are particularly helpful for female athletes, as they help balance estrogen levels in the body and protect against osteoporosis by increasing bone mass. Soy beans also contain B-vitamins, which play a role in helping the body cope with stress.

NUTRIENTS

Vitamins B1, B2, B3, B5, B6, E, K, beta-carotene, folate; calcium, copper, iodine, iron, magnesium, manganese, phosphorus, potassium, selenium, zinc

BANANA, AVOCADO, AND SOY SMOOTHIE
serves 2

1 ripe banana, peeled
1 avocado, peeled and pitted
3½oz. silken tofu
1¾ cups soy milk
a generous sprinkling
   almond slivers

Whiz together the banana, avocado, tofu, and soy milk in a blender until smooth. Sprinkle with the almond slivers and serve immediately.

garlic

Eating garlic guarantees extra protection for overworked joints and helps keep the heart healthy, too.

Exercise places increased strain on the joints and can sometimes set up an inflammatory response in the body. Consuming a clove of garlic a day has been proven to counteract inflammation. A sulfur compound in garlic known as allicin has been found to aid weight loss and to protect against heart disease by preventing fatty deposits forming inside the arteries. Its selenium and zinc content boost immunity.

NUTRIENTS
Vitamins B1, B6, C, folate; calcium, copper, iron, manganese, phosphorus, potassium, selenium, sulfur, zinc

GARLIC-MUSHROOM SALAD

4 garlic cloves, crushed
12 flat mushrooms
3 tbsp. olive oil
4 handfuls arugula leaves
4oz. feta cheese

In a pan, gently fry the garlic and both sides of the mushrooms in the oil. Arrange the arugula on four plates. Put 3 mushrooms on each pile of leaves and crumble the cheese over. Serve immediately.

ginger

With its great pain-relieving and circulation-boosting properties, ginger is a useful addition to any athlete's diet.

Ginger is useful for anyone feeling sluggish because it is stimulating and promotes detoxification by increasing perspiration and circulation. Recognized by scientists as a fast-acting cure for nausea of all kinds, fresh ginger also contains anti-inflammatory compounds called gingerols, which suppress the substances that trigger pain and swelling in the joints. In addition, it is particularly rich in the mineral zinc— essential for a healthy immune system.

NUTRIENTS
Vitamin B3, B6, C, E, folate; calcium, copper, iron, magnesium, manganese, phosphorus, potassium, selenium, zinc

GINGERADE
serves 2

1 tbsp. sugar
2oz. ginger root, peeled and cut into ½-in. chunks
1 cup sparkling mineral water
juice of ½ lemon

Place the sugar, ginger root, and 1 cup water in a pan and bring to a boil. Reduce the heat, cover, and simmer 10 minutes. Leave to cool and strain to remove the ginger pieces. Stir in the sparkling mineral water, add the lemon juice, and serve with ice.

For a postgame or postrace reviver, pour hot water on grated ginger and drink as a tea.

cinnamon

CINNAMON FACTS
*Cinnamon is a spice made from the inner bark of the *Cinnamomum zeylanicum* tree.

*The bark is stripped from the tree and left to dry in the sun. While drying, it rolls up into a quill (sold as a cinnamon stick). Some of the quills are then ground into a powder.

*Cinnamon is one of the oldest-known spices. It was mentioned in ancient Chinese writings 2,700 years ago and features several times in the Bible.

*Ceylon cinnamon has a lighter, sweeter and more delicate flavor than the Indonesian variety.

This fragrant spice provids a healthy alternative for athletes who find it difficult to resist unhealthy sugary snacks.

STABILIZES BLOOD SUGAR
Research has shown that compounds in cinnamon stabilize blood-sugar levels, which, in turn, prevents mood swings and dips in blood sugar post-exercise—a time when even the most health-conscious athlete might be tempted to succumb to calorie-laden chocolate and sweets. As little as half a teaspoonful a day—sprinkled on oatmeal for breakfast or used to sweeten a cup of herbal tea—can make a difference and, say scientists, even help to control type 2 diabetes.

APPLE AND CINNAMON OATMEAL

2 cinnamon sticks
5 whole cloves
2 tsp. sugar
2 apples, peeled and sliced
1 cup instant rolled oats

In a large pan, bring 3 cups water to a boil. Reduce the heat, add the cinnamon, cloves, sugar, and apple, and simmer 10 minutes. Remove the spices, stir in the oats, and serve.

PREVENTS YEAST INFECTIONS

Cinnamon also has antibacterial and antifungal properties that have been found to inhibit organisms such as *Candida albicans*, a yeastlike fungus responsible for causing vaginal infections.

Cinnamon's distinct smell works directly on the brain to increase alertness.

CINNAMON TEA *serves 2*

4 tsp. black tea
4 cinnamon sticks
1 lemon, sliced

Place all the ingredients in a pan and cover with four cups freshly boiled water. Steep 5 minutes, then pour the tea through a strainer into four cups and serve.

parsley

Balance fluid levels in the body by scattering one of the world's most popular culinary herbs over salads and into hot dishes.

The richest herbal source of the mineral potassium, parsley is a natural diuretic, encouraging the excretion of sodium and water. This helps balance fluid levels in the body, which can be disturbed by exercise. Curly and broadleaf Italian parsley are both excellent sources of the fatigue-fighting duo, iron and vitamin C. Both have been used traditionally to improve arthritic conditions.

NUTRIENTS
Vitamins A, B1, B3, B5, C, E, K, folate; calcium, copper, iodine, iron, magnesium, manganese, phosphorus, potassium, selenium, zinc

PARSLEY SAUCE

2 tbsp. butter
1 tbsp. all-purpose flour
1½ cups milk
2 tbsp. heavy cream
juice and zest of ½ lemon
4 tbsp. finely chopped
  parsley
freshly ground black pepper
grilled white fish, to serve

In a small pan, gently melt the butter, then stir in the flour to form a smooth paste. Gradually add the milk, bring to a boil, and reduce the heat. Simmer 3 minutes, whisking constantly. Add the cream, lemon, and parsley and season with pepper. Serve over grilled white fish.

tofu

One of the best vegetarian forms of protein for athletes, tofu works well in everything from smoothies to stir-fries.

Also known as bean curd, tofu is a versatile, low-fat food that's jam-packed with nutrients. Like all soy products, it is rich in phytoestrogens, which help regulate hormone levels, and calcium to build strong bones. Tofu is a good source of omega-3 fatty acids and fiber, which both help stave off food cravings. It also contains an isoflavone called genistein, which seems to promote fat loss by reducing the size and number of fat cells.

NUTRIENTS
Vitamins A, K; calcium, copper, iron, magnesium, manganese, phosphorus, potassium, selenium; omega-3 and -6 essential fatty acids

BLUEBERRY AND TOFU MOUSSE

7oz. silken tofu
1¾ cups blueberries
1 cup finely ground almonds
1 tsp. cinnamon
1 tsp. lemon juice
2 tsp. toasted, slivered almonds

Blend the tofu and blueberries in a food processor. Add the ground almonds, cinnamon, and lemon juice and mix well. Spoon into four bowls, sprinkle with the almonds, and serve.

Soft tofu blends easily in smoothies and desserts; firm tofu works well in main meals.

miso

Miso does more than just add flavor to soups and stews—it notches up their nutrient rankings, too.

A naturally fermented paste, miso is made from soy beans, sea salt, and a yeast mold called *koji*. A handy cupboard staple, it is ideal for spicing up soups, sauces, and stews. Miso is an excellent source of protein, and boasts a host of minerals to enhance an athlete's performance, including manganese, which strengthens nerves, bones and muscles, and phosphorus, necessary for the metabolism of fats, protein, and glucose.

NUTRIENTS

Vitamins B1, B2, B3, B5, B6, K, beta-carotene, folate; calcium, copper, iron, magnesium, manganese, phosphorus, potassium, selenium, sodium, zinc

Dark miso contains more protein and essential fatty acids than lighter varieties.

MISO SANDWICH SPREAD

1 tbsp. miso
1 tbsp. tahini
1 garlic clove, crushed

Mix all the ingredients together in a small bowl. Use as a spread on warm crusty wholewheat bread or as a tasty substitute for butter in sandwiches.

balsamic vinegar

Thanks to its alkalizing effect, balsamic vinegar is a useful ingredient for fitness lovers who are prone to muscle cramps.

Originally from the Modena province of Italy, this dark brown, syrupy vinegar is made from reduced grape juice aged in wooden casks. Like all vinegars, balsamic is bursting with enzymes and trace minerals that help balance the body's acid–alkaline levels. It is especially rich in the disease-fighting phytochemicals found in grapes, which become even more potent during its fermentation process.

NUTRIENTS

Vitamins B1, B2, B6, C, E, beta-carotene; calcium, iron, magnesium, manganese, phosphorus, potassium, selenium, silica, sulfur, zinc

TANGY SALAD DRESSING

4 tbsp. balsamic vinegar
juice and zest of 1 orange
juice and zest of 1 lime
1 tbsp. mustard
1 tbsp. olive oil
2 garlic cloves, crushed

Place all the ingredients in a screw-top jar and shake well to combine. Store in the refrigerator for up to 1 week.

ailments directory

ANEMIA

This condition occurs when there is a decrease in the amount of oxygen-carrying hemoglobin in our red blood cells. Symptoms include feeling tired all the time, weakness, pale skin, breathlessness, and pale inner lower eyelids. Eating foods rich in iron and vitamin B12 can help combat anemia.

Foods to eat:

Plum (p.12); Broccoli (p.37); Chard (p.39); Beef (p.62); Lamb (p.63); Amaranth (p.93); Quinoa (p.96); Lentil (p.102)

ATHLETE'S FOOT

Athlete's foot is a common fungal infection characterized by itchy dry patches of skin between the toes that sometimes split open. It's highly contagious, often thriving on the damp floors of changing rooms and communal showers. Help your body to fight it off by avoiding refined sugar products and by limiting your consumption of yeast products, such as bread, alcohol, and yeast extract.

Foods to eat:

Eggplant (p.46); Yogurt (p.71); Garlic (p.112); Ginger (p.113); Cinnamon (p.114); Balsamic vinegar (p.119)

BLISTERS

A common sports ailment, blisters often form on the feet and heels. They are caused by friction on the outer layers of skin forming fluid-filled sacks to protect the inner layers of skin from more damage. To prevent them, wear well-fitting trainers and socks. To help heal them, eat foods rich in vitamins C and K, which both speed up the healing process.

Foods to eat:

Star fruit (p.16); Goji berry (p.24); Chard (p.39); Bok choy (p.40); Egg (p.73); Oats (p.94)

CRAMP

Cramp is the sudden uncontrolled contraction of a muscle, often in the thigh or calf. The exact cause is unknown, but it's thought

overexertion from exercise, muscle fatigue and excessive sweating (which depletes the body of minerals, such as sodium, potassium, magnesium, and calcium), can all play a part. Anyone prone to regular cramps is wise to eat foods loaded with these important minerals.

Foods to eat:

Pear (p.10); Date (p.19); Papaya (p.21); Butternut squash (p.34); Shrimp (p.56); Chicken (p.66); Cashew (p.80); Aduki bean (p.104)

DEHYDRATION

During exercise, the body loses fluids through perspiration. The amount depends on how hard and long you train for, as well as the surrounding temperature and humidity.

Losing the equivalent of two percent of your body weight in sweat results in a 10 to 20 percent drop in performance (or aerobic capacity). Severe dehydration can lead to vomiting and heat exhaustion. That's why it's recommended that athletes drink enough fluids every day to guarantee they need to urinate every two to four hours so the urine is lightly colored and copious. The American College of Sports Medicine recommends drinking ⅔ to ¾ cup water every 15 to 30 minutes during a workout. And an athlete should drink at least 2 quarts of liquid during the course of a day. You can also improve your hydration by eating foods with a high water content.

Foods to eat:

Plum (p.12); Peach (p.13); Lemon (p.14); Orange (p.15); Mango (p.20); Lychee (p.23); Milk (p.70); Coconut (p.83)

DEPRESSION (MILD)

Characterized by tearfulness, anxiety, and feelings of hopelessness, mild depression is a condition experienced by one in four people at some stage in their lives. Cutting out alcohol, cigarettes, and sugary foods and eating those high in omega-3 fatty acids and B-vitamins is thought to help. Exercise is also known to increase the feel-good factor.

Foods to eat:

Salmon (p.50); Tuna (p.51); Mackerel (p.53); Walnut (p.74); Quinoa (p.96); Spelt (p.98); Brown rice (p.100)

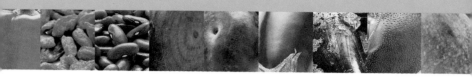

HEART DISEASE

One of the main causes of heart disease is the blockage of arteries by cholesterol. Following an exercise regime and eating monounsaturated fats (found in olive oil, nuts, seeds, and fish) instead of saturated fats (found in animal products and processed foods) can make a dramatic difference to your heart health.

Foods to eat:

Avocado (p.25); Olive (p.26); Salmon (p.50); Tuna (p.51); Mackerel (p.53); Pistachio (p.78); Sunflower seed (p.87); Peanut (p.106)

HIGH BLOOD PRESSURE

Hypertension, or high blood pressure, means the heart has to work harder to pump blood around the body, and increases the risk of heart disease and stroke. You can bring it down through exercise, stress reduction, and losing excess weight. It also helps if you avoid high-fat and salt-laden dishes and opt instead for foods loaded with magnesium, vitamin C, essential fatty acids, and fiber.

Foods to eat:

Orange (p.15); Goji berry (p.24); Broccoli (p.37); Mushroom (p.41); Trout (p.49); Oats (p.94); Lentil (p.102); Edamame (p.105)

INSOMNIA

An inability to drop off to sleep or a pattern of waking up during the night can lead to health problems such as fatigue, irritability, and lower levels of concentration. Studies show exercise and physical activity increase our mental alertness for four hours afterward, so avoiding evening workouts can help prevent insomnia. Stimulants, such as coffee and chocolate, can also interrupt sleep patterns if you consume them less than five hours before bed. Instead, encourage sleep with foods rich in B-vitamins, magnesium, calcium, and the amino acid, tryptophan.

Foods to eat:

Banana (p.11); Fig (p.18); Date (p.19); Chard (p.39); Sardine (p.52); Turkey (p.65); Milk (p.70); Egg (p.73)

JOINT PROBLEMS

Regular exercise can place a strain on the joints. For example, knee pain is a

common running injury. It's possible to protect joints from injury and wear and tear by maintaining the correct weight for your height and by alternating periods of heavy activity with periods of rest to avoid repetitive stress on your joints. Research also shows eating foods rich in essential fatty acids can help protect the cartilage cells that facilitate joint movement.

Foods to eat:

Olive (p.26); Salmon (p.50); Mackerel (p.53); Walnut (p.74); Flaxseed (p.85); Wild rice (p.101); Garlic (p.112); Ginger (p.113)

OBESITY

You are described as being obese if your body weight reaches 20 percent above the recommended maximum for your height. An exercise programme coupled with a nutrient-dense diet is key to shedding the extra weight.

Foods to eat:

Lettuce (p.28); Bell pepper (p.29); Yogurt (p.71); Almond (p.75); Pine nut (p.77); Kidney bean (p.109); Tofu (p.117)

OSTEOPOROSIS

Osteoporosis causes bones to become weak so you are more prone to fractures and breaks. Eating foods rich in calcium, as well as phosphorus and magnesium, can help to prevent the disease. Making sure you spend plenty of time outside also helps, as the sun triggers the production of vitamin D, which helps to turn the calcium you eat into bone.

Foods to eat:

Fig (p.18); Onion (p.31); Sardine (p.52); Milk (p.70); Yogurt (p.71); Cheese (p.72); Sesame seed (p.86); Tofu (p.117)

POSTVIRAL FATIGUE (M.E.)

Although the specific cause of postviral fatigue is still unknown, it often follows on from a viral illness and is more likely to occur in athletes who overtrain. This chronic condition is characterized by low energy levels and poor concentration. Eating plenty of immunity-boosting fruit and vegetables can help to alleviate the symptoms.

Foods to eat:

Star fruit (p.16); Guava (p.22); Goji berry (p.24); Bell pepper (p.29); Beet (p.30); Carrot (p.33); Garlic (p.112)

glossary

Adrenalin A hormone released in response to stress that boosts the supply of oxygen and glucose to the brain and muscles.

Allicin A compound in garlic that has potent antibacterial and antifungal activities.

Amino acids Compounds, either made by the body or found in the diet, which are involved in processes such as the formation of neurotransmitters in the brain.

Antibacterial A substance that destroys or inhibits the growth of bacteria.

Antifungal A substance that destroys or inhibits the growth of fungi.

Anti-inflammatory A substance that prevents or reduces inflammation.

Antioxidants Compounds in fruit and vegetables that fight free radicals, preventing cell degeneration and decay.

Arginine An organic compound found in animal proteins.

Beta-carotene A fat-soluble vitamin found as carotenoids in plant foods, which the body converts into vitamin A.

Betaine A phytonutrient used by the liver to produce choline, a compound that promotes muscle growth.

Blood sugar The form in which fuel from food is carried in the blood to provide energy to cells.

Calorie A measurement of the energy the body gets from food; the body needs calories as "fuel" to perform all its functions.

Capsaicin An active component found in bell peppers and chilis.

Carbohydrate Starchy or sweet food, which provides the body with energy.

Cartilage A type of dense connective tissue that cushions

bones at the joints to absorb shock and prevent them from grating together.

Cholesterol A waxy substance found in red blood cells.

Choline A B-complex vitamin that is a constituent of lecithin; it is essential in the metabolism of fat, for good heart health and in the regulation of mood, appetite, behavior, and memory.

Chondroitin sulfate A complex molecule that gives cartilage the elastic, spongelike quality joints need to act as shock absorbers between bones.

Citric acid A plant acid that's an important component in the flavor of citrus fruit.

Cortisol A hormone produced by the adrenal glands, often referred to as the "stress hormone."

Cruciferous A type of vegetable that's exceptionally rich in beneficial nutrients; includes cauliflower, Brussels sprouts, and many dark green leafy vegetables.

Crustacean Seawater or freshwater creatures that have a hard outer shell and no backbone; includes lobsters, shrimps, crayfish, and crabs.

Detoxification The body's natural process of eliminating toxic substances.

Dipeptides Muscle-building substances found in meat, especially turkey.

Diuretic Encourages the production of urine.

Docosahexaemoic acid (DHA) An omega-3 fatty acid found in fish.

Electrolyte A substance containing free ions, such as sodium, potassium, calcium, and magnesium; commonly found in sports drinks to help replenish the body's fluid levels.

Endurance The body's ability to exercise with minimal fatigue.

Enzyme A protein that facilitates the body's chemical reactions.

Essential amino acids Organic compounds that form the building blocks of protein and are vital to human health; the body can't produce them so they must be supplied by the diet.

Essential Fatty Acids (EFAs) Polyunsaturated fats the body can't manufacture that are vital for healthy blood, skin, nerves, and the functioning of the immune system.

Fat One of three food groups, which we need to include in our diet; used for numerous purposes including cell maintenance and absorption of certain vitamins.

Fiber Plant matter in food that the body does not absorb, but that aids the process of digestion.

Flavonoids An umbrella term for the anti-inflammatory antioxidants found in many natural foods.

Folic acid Vitamin B9

Free radicals Highly reactive molecules that are damaging to the body and are linked to causing degenerative diseases, such as cancer, as well as speeding up the aging process.

Fructose A simple sugar found in honey and fruits.

Gingerol A source of spiciness in fresh ginger root.

Glucose The simplest form of sugar.

Glucosinolates Compounds found in vegetables in the cabbage family that have anticancer properties.

Gluten A protein found mainly in wheat, and in smaller amounts in barley and rye.

Glycemic Index (GI) A system devised for ranking foods according to their effect on blood-sugar levels—foods with a high GI cause blood sugar to rise more quickly than medium or low GI foods.

Glycogen The form in which energy is stored in the muscles for later use.

Hesperin A cholesterol-lowering flavonoid with antioxidant and anti-inflammatory properties that is found in citrus fruit.

Homocysteine An amino acid used by the body in cellular metabolism and the manufacture of proteins; high levels of this substance have been found to be linked to an increased risk of heart disease and stroke.

Hormone A chemical substance released by the endocrine glands such as the thyroid and adrenal glands, and the ovaries, which travels through the bloodstream and affects the function of cells in other parts of the body.

Hull The dry outer covering of a fruit, seed, or nut.

Hydrate To consume enough water to restore or maintain the body's fluid balance.

Insulin A hormone that regulates the body's blood-sugar levels.

Isoflavones Plant hormones that mimic the hormone estrogen in the body.

Lactobacilli Friendly bacteria that live in the gut and support the immune system; bio-yogurt is a good source.

Lactose A natural sugar found in milk.

Lecithin A yellow phospholipid essential for the metabolism of fats; found in egg yolk and many plant and animal cells.

Leptin A hormone that plays a key role in regulating energy intake and expenditure; controls appetite and metabolism.

Lignans Antioxidant chemicals found in some plants, especially flaxseed; similar in structure to the hormone estrogen, they mimic its actions in the body.

Lutein An antioxidant carotenoid important for eye health.

Lysine An essential amino acid found in proteins; important for growth, tissue repair, and the production of hormones, enzymes and antibodies.

Metabolism The process in the body that converts food into energy.

Mineral An inorganic chemical element, such as calcium, iron, potassium, sodium, or zinc, required by the body for biochemical reactions; essential for optimal health.

Mononsaturated fat The healthiest type of fat found in food, which can help to lower cholesterol.

Niacin Vitamin B3

Nutrient A substance that can be metabolized in the body to provide energy and build tissue.

Oleic acid An omega-9 essential fatty acid, found in various animal and plant food source, especially olives and olive oil.

Organic Food made according to strict production standards; crops are grown without the use of conventional pesticides or artificial fertilizers, free from human or industrial contamination, and processed without ionizing radiation or food additives; animals are reared without antibiotics or growth hormones, and are fed healthily.

Osteoclasts The cells that break down bone.

Oxidation Exposure to oxygen that causes cell degeneration and decay.

Pantothenic acid Vitamin B5

Papain An enzyme found in papaya that aids the digestion of protein.

Pectin A type of soluble fibre in fruit and vegetables that lowers cholesterol levels.

Phospholipids Fats required for cell membranes and a healthy brain; found in eggs.

Phytoestrogen A plant compound that has similar, yet weaker, effects to those of the hormone oestrogen.

Phytonutrient A nutrient derived from a plant source.

Prebiotics Nondigestible fibers that are the energy source for the friendly bacteria in the colon.

Protein One of three food groups needed in our diet; essential for the growth and repair of muscle and tissue.

Pyridoxine Vitamin B6

Quercertin An anti-inflammatory flavonoid; found in onions.

Rancid Having a rank taste and/or smell, commonly owing to the oxidation of oils or fats in food.

Resveratrol An antioxidant found in fruit and red wine, which has anticancer, antiviral and anti-inflammatory properties.

Riboflavin Vitamin B2

Rutin A flavonoid antioxidant found in buckwheat, that helps strengthen the blood vessels and fight heart disease.

Satiety The feeling of fullness or the disappearance of hunger after a meal.

Serotonin A chemical produced by nerve cells in the brain that lifts the mood; also found in some foods.

Thiamine Vitamin B1

Thyroid One of the largest endocrine glands in the body, found in the neck; it controls how quickly the body burns energy and makes proteins and how sensitive the body is to hormones.

Tryptophan An amino acid that the brain converts into the "feelgood" chemical, serotonin.

Vitamins Fat-soluble and water-soluble organic substances, such as beta-carotene, that are obtained naturally from plant and animal foods; essential in minute amounts for the normal growth and activity of the body.

Wholegrain Cereal grains that retain the bran and germ of the plant, such as whole wheat flour, brown rice and oatmeal.

index

Author's acknowledgments

Sarah would like to thank her husband, Anthony, and her three sons, Harry, Jonah, and Luke, for their unfailing love and support during the writing of this book.

Publishers' acknowledgments

Thanks to The Fish Society (www.thefishsociety.co.uk) for providing crayfish and cod roe for the photo shoot.